OXFORD-BIRMINGHAM

Portrait of a Famous Route

BOB PIXTON

RUNPAST PUBLISHING

© 2006 Bob Pixton and Runpast Publishing

Published by Runpast Publishing, 10 Kingscote Grove, Cheltenham, Gloucestershire GL51 6JX

Typesetting and reproduction by Viners Wood Associates
Printed in England by The Amadeus Press Ltd., Cleckheaton

ISBN 1 870754 66 2

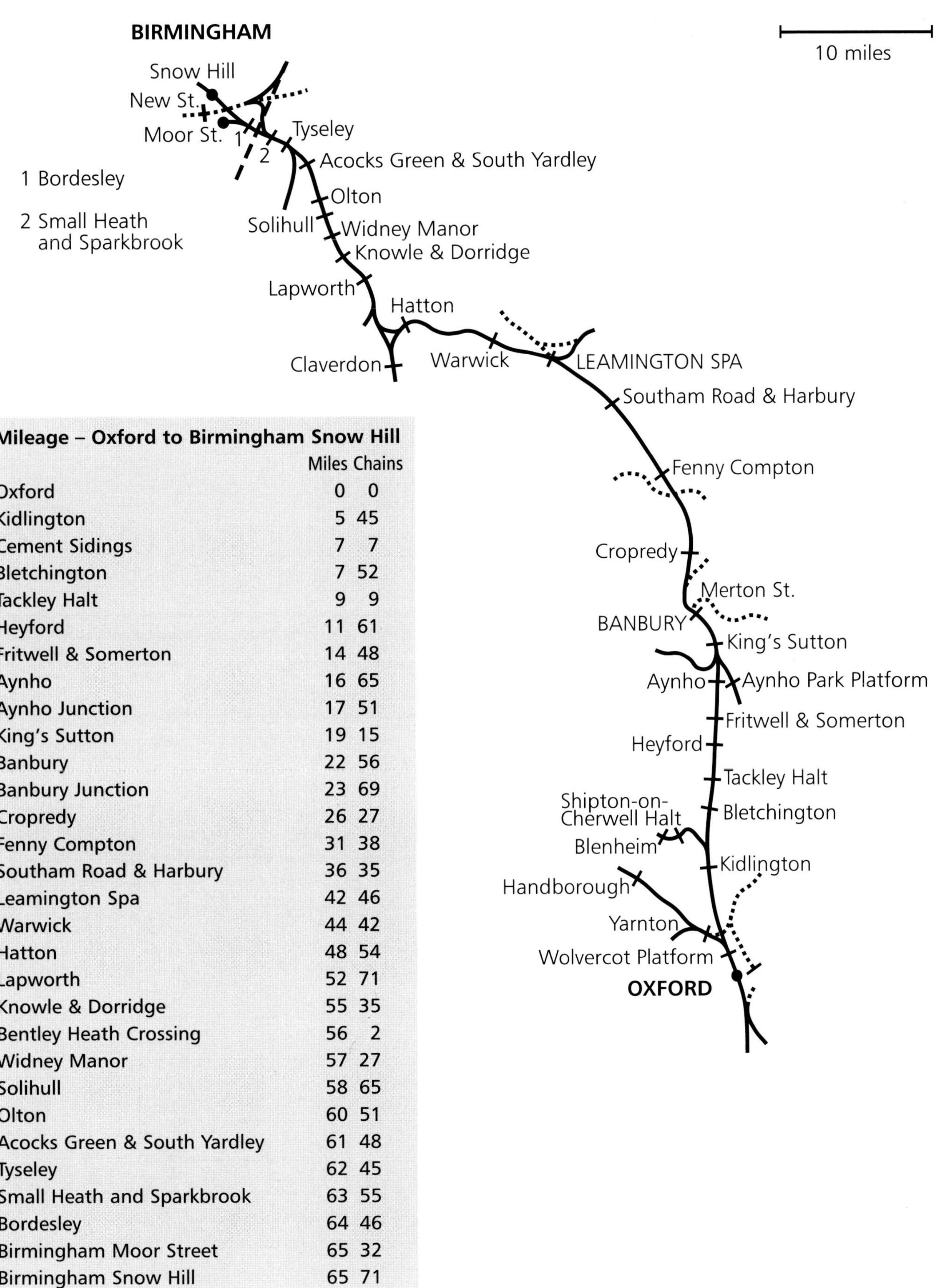

Mileage – Oxford to Birmingham Snow Hill

	Miles	Chains
Oxford	0	0
Kidlington	5	45
Cement Sidings	7	7
Bletchington	7	52
Tackley Halt	9	9
Heyford	11	61
Fritwell & Somerton	14	48
Aynho	16	65
Aynho Junction	17	51
King's Sutton	19	15
Banbury	22	56
Banbury Junction	23	69
Cropredy	26	27
Fenny Compton	31	38
Southam Road & Harbury	36	35
Leamington Spa	42	46
Warwick	44	42
Hatton	48	54
Lapworth	52	71
Knowle & Dorridge	55	35
Bentley Heath Crossing	56	2
Widney Manor	57	27
Solihull	58	65
Olton	60	51
Acocks Green & South Yardley	61	48
Tyseley	62	45
Small Heath and Sparkbrook	63	55
Bordesley	64	46
Birmingham Moor Street	65	32
Birmingham Snow Hill	65	71

Kidlington, 20 August 1966. Despite BR Western Region's avowed intention to be rid of steam by the beginning of 1966, Oxford continued to see steam locos, like this LMR based 9F No.92002 – an ex-WR loco shedded at an ex-GW depot, Tyseley – with the 10. 45am Bournemouth to Newcastle, which the engine had worked up from the Southern Region. Cross-country summer trains routed via Banbury and the former Great Central Railway through Leicester were still quite steamy that summer – but change was about to occur as two weeks after this picture was taken the line from Banbury to Woodford Halse was closed and these services were diverted to traverse Leamington Spa and Birmingham New Street. The down goods loop is still in use, but the loop siding was taken up in 1965, though the loading gauge remains.

Cox

Introduction

When the route from Oxford to Birmingham was first proposed in the late 1840s it would have traversed very rural areas of England and, even today, not a lot has changed in the southern part. For the first fifty years of the line's existence much of Oxfordshire suffered from a population reduction – it was only the bigger towns like Banbury (population 8,206 in 1851) and Oxford that grew, modestly. It is no surprise that two of the main employers in Banbury – Samuelson & Co and Barrows – were manufacturers of agricultural machinery emphasising the rural domination of the area, about half a million acres. But there was massive growth in industry and commerce around the northern part of the line, within easy reach of Birmingham.

So the line evolved as an important route between the latter city and London, becoming part of the GWR's Northern Division. From Birmingham, the Great Western was able to access Wolverhampton, Shrewsbury, Chester, North Wales, Birkenhead, Liverpool and Manchester, while important places such as Banbury, Leamington, Warwick and Solihull were served *en route* from Oxford. The route started off as broad gauge, but became mixed, with trains running on both gauges for some years – see the timetable reproduced on page 78 of this book. The GWR faced stiff competition from the London & North Western Railway for traffic between London and Birmingham and the north, with the latter railway often bettering its rival in terms of speed and frequency of trains. However the Great Western gradually rose to the challenge. In his book 'The **Great** Great Western' W J Scott enthused in 1902 concerning the Northern line : 'Here the transformation scene is at its brightest. Where, twenty-three years ago, there was a meagre service, made up mostly of 'slow fasts' with one solitary up express from Wolverhampton, there is now the most brilliant group of high-speed expresses on the whole system – one of the finest in Great Britain, in fact... . In the summer of 1891 great additions were made to the service, and the bettering then begun has lately – under pressure of North-Western competition – been brought to a much higher pitch, but the end is not yet.' With the opening of the direct line via Princes Risborough in 1910, services from London to Birmingham were improved even more, though Oxford lost some through trains. But the earlier linking at Banbury to the Great Central Railway had already brought a lot of new north–south cross-country traffic through Oxford, so the line was still kept very busy. Commuter traffic was particularly important at the Birmingham end, with the railway enabling the well-heeled to live in leafy places like Solihull rather than the grime of inner city industrial areas. A new terminus was opened at Moor Street Birmingham to cater for the burgeoning local traffic which had increased with the opening of the North Warwickshire line. The main stations along the route all started off with train sheds to protect passengers, some lasted longer than others. Both Oxford's and Leamington's had gone long before the start of the twentieth century, Birmingham's were replaced in 1907 and Banbury's in the mid 1950s. Oxford's wooden buildings were replaced by similar ones in the 1890s, Birmingham's brick buildings were altered in the early 1900s. Although being in the Anglo-Italian style, Leamington's was rebuilt in the 1930s while the dilapidated and worn out wooden buildings at Banbury were eventually replaced in the mid 1950s, delayed by the war. Oxford's wooden buildings were swept away in the 1970s, with the current station dating from the early 1990s.

There were large yards at Banbury and Bordesley to sort and make up freight trains. Engine sheds at Oxford, Banbury, Leamington and Tyseley provided motive power and servicing facilities, with the latter also having heavy workshop capabilities. Oxford and Banbury saw locomotives from other railway companies on a daily basis, while there was a time when engines from the Southern Railway worked through to Birmingham via Oxford.

The route between Oxford and Birmingham was certainly important enough to see significant improvements in the 1920s and 1930s with two tracks widened out to four and stations between Birmingham and Leamington being enlarged. But the decision in the 1950s to electrify the North-Western line between London and Birmingham led to a big reduction of passenger services on the old GWR routes. There was actually an increase in services from Snow Hill to Paddington to compensate for the disruption on the North-Western while the modernisation work was underway in the late 1950s and early 1960s, but then the decline set in with closures and track reductions. The glory that was Birmingham Snow Hill was lost forever when the last main line services were diverted to New Street in March 1967, with just a few local trains using it after that date. When these too were taken off, dereliction was followed by total destruction in 1977. It has of course since reopened on a smaller scale for commuter services, with long distance trains still using a very crowded New Street. New through platforms were also constructed at Moor Street, which had otherwise fallen into disuse, though restoration work at the terminus there has taken place in recent years ready for a possible reopening. While the Princes Risborough cut off is now basically a secondary route, though still providing an alternative Birmingham–London service, the old line north from Oxford is thriving with lack of capacity being its main problem. Long distance passenger services are much more frequent than in steam days, with a seemingly constant stream of cross-country trains fighting with container freights for a path between Oxford and Birmingham. With preserved steam depots at both Didcot and Tyseley, the line is still able to provide a link with the past by hosting a goodly number of steam-hauled specials, with each locomotive's performance on the stiff climb up Hatton bank eagerly anticipated, and where lineside photographers still gather as in days past.

Contents

Oxford

Due to objections from the colleges in town, Oxford originally had to make do with a horse-drawn coach connection with the Great Western Railway's London to Bristol line at Steventon. However, over time these objections were worn down by the obvious advantages of having a rail link. The Oxford Railway was a project funded by the GWR to construct a broad gauge line from its main line at Didcot to a wooden station south of the river in the Grandpound area. This railway was just over nine and a half miles long and opened on 12 June 1844.

An Act of Parliament dated 4 August 1845 allowed the Oxford & Rugby Railway – absorbed by the GWR from 4 May 1846 – to build a connection from just south of Oxford station to join the London & Birmingham Railway at Rugby. As the latter place was the southern extremity of the Midland Counties Railway with its connections via Derby to the eastern side of England, the GWR reasoned that much traffic would flow along its lines. The Oxford & Rugby was eventually opened as a single broad gauge line from Oxford Millstream Junction to Banbury on 2 September 1850 – the extension to Rugby was never built. For the period to 1 October 1852 when the new station north of Botley Road was opened, Banbury trains used the first Oxford station, reversing at Millstream Junction on the main line. In the meantime, the Birmingham & Oxford Junction Railway had, since 3 August 1846, been given permission to meet the Oxford & Rugby at Fenny Compton north of Banbury. Again this company was absorbed by the GWR, in 1848, and the line from Banbury via Leamington and Hatton opened to Birmingham on 1 October 1852.

On 20 May 1851 the Buckinghamshire Junction Railway (later London & North Western Railway) opened a station at Oxford Rewley Road as the terminus of a line from Bletchley constructed as 'standard' gauge only.

From 4 June 1853, the Oxford, Worcester & Wolverhampton Railway ran trains on the standard (or narrow) gauge, using the new Oxford station and joining the GWR line at Wolvercot Junction. This change in gauge was to be the cause of the GWR and OWW, which the GWR had nurtured and financed, falling out. Although the line from Worcester was mixed gauge it is doubtful if any real broad gauge services ran along it. In 1854 the LNWR opened a connecting curve from their line at Oxford Road Junction to meet the OWW at Yarnton. This meant that virtually all the OWW's London traffic could travel narrow gauge along the GWR's rival, while the LNWR also ran through trains from London to Wolverhampton along the route.

'Narrow' gauge lines were laid south of Oxford from 1856 although it was not until 1861 that the GWR's first London to Birmingham train ran completely on the 'narrow' gauge (the GWR term at that time for standard gauge). Details from working time tables dated 1862 are reproduced on page 78 of this book and show both broad and narrow gauge trains between Oxford and Birmingham. The original section from Oxford was doubled and so two tracks extended between the two places. One consequence was the cessation of the Euston to Wolverhampton services: the curve from Yarnton Loop towards Bletchley was severed before being finally lifted. But a west to south link was laid from the loop to the LNWR line enabling OWW trains to use either Oxford station – in fact most used the GWR one as this was more popular with passengers who needed connections with London trains.

However, with Oxford's GWR goods depots being south of the new station at St. Aldgate and, chiefly, at the old station accessed from Millstream Junction, the OWW opted to use the LNWR goods depot at Rewley Road to save it the cost of laying a third rail, leading to a further souring of relationships with the GWR. But in 1861 the GWR took over the West Midland Railway, a constituent of which was the OWW, so such differences were gradually overcome.

For well over fifty years from October 1852 the GWR ran its London to Birmingham services through Oxford. The opening of a cut off via Princes Risborough in 1910 reduced the journey time by around twenty minutes, and could have cast Oxford into the role of a backwater. (Gloucester suffered the same fate when the Severn Tunnel was opened.) Nevertheless, while heavy Birkenhead expresses went along the new direct line so that two hour timings between London and Birmingham could be achieved, many GWR services to the West Midlands still passed by way of Reading, Oxford and Leamington. If speed was the criterion then the direct line was best but for serving big intermediate towns, then the 'old main line' was still important. Thus two Birmingham trains from platform 3 at Paddington – at 8.40am via Oxford and at 9.10am via Bicester – both conveyed passengers to Leamington, with the later train getting passengers there a good half hour before the earlier one. An increasing number of cross-country trains between the south coast and the East Midlands and north via the Great Central Railway link at Banbury opened in 1898 also helped to ensure that Oxford remained an important station on the railway system.

Thanks to a 1940s wartime connection, ex-LNWR passenger trains were diverted to the ex-GWR station from 1 October 1951 with Rewley Road closing from that date. The wooden buildings are now part preserved and used at Quainton Road in Buckinghamshire.

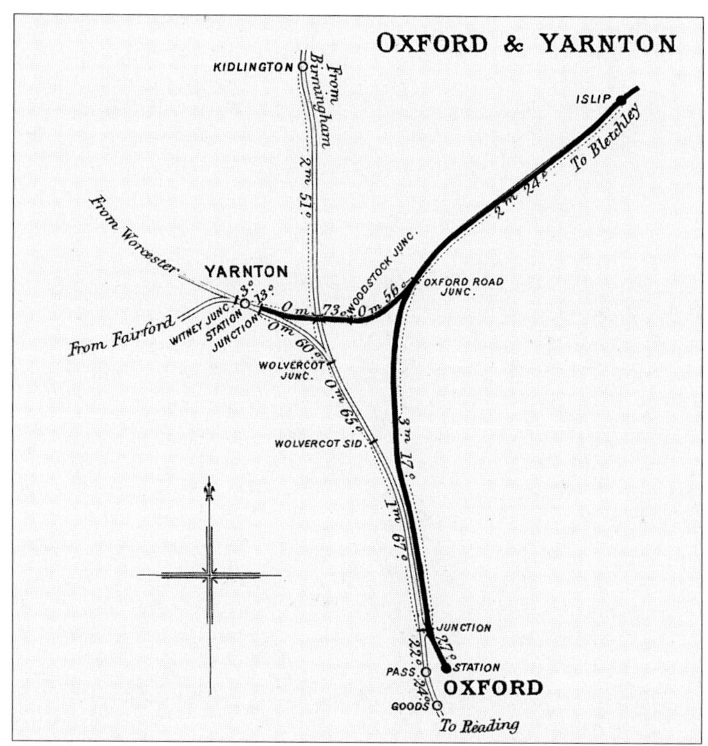

Above: **South of Oxford, Kennington, early 1950s**. Six years after opening, the original Oxford Railway made a junction - Millstream - with the new Oxford & Rugby Railway in 1850 around here. Since those early days the old station had closed and the main line quadrupled. Heading south on the up main line is 2-6-2T No. 4404. It has just passed a signal which had indicator boards telling the driver which route he was to take at Kennington Junction, a short distance ahead. The bracket signal on the left of the picture allowed trains on the up fast line to pass onto the Thame and Princes Risborough branch. The apparatus for single line working can just be made out to the right of the engine. On the down side, the bracket signal was for the new Hinksey yards. Adjacent to the bridge in the background, Abingdon Road, a halt existed between 1 February 1908 and 22 March 1915.   *Author's collection*

Below: **Hinksey Yard, circa 1960**. Looking south sees an express from the Southern Region being signalled to stop at Oxford station. To the left above the coaches is Hinksey Pool, a set of gravel pits whose excavation provided material for the trackbed of the Oxford & Rugby Railway. The far bank is the approximate position of the original line to Oxford's first station. In the background, where the lines curve to the right, was the site of another short-lived halt, Hinksey. The main lines were quadrupled as part of wartime activity to reduce traffic bottlenecks on the way to the south coast in the build-up to the 'D' Day landings and afterwards. Constructed at the same time were the sorting sidings. They consisted of a down yard, closest in the picture, and an up yard beyond. Essentially, both had ten dead end sidings and associated loops to facilitate train movements. The line almost directly beneath the photographer is the up reception with the line on the extreme right being the down loop.   *Author's collection*

Above: **'Cemetery' footbridge, 1950s.** South of the bridge an ex-LNWR 'G' class 0-8-0 No.49452 is waiting in one of the three loops adjacent to Oxford goods shed. The empty wagons may have come from the goods yard or from the Southern Gas Board works whose access was a short distance beyond the bracket signal in the background. The train would probably be awaiting a suitable gap in passenger traffic to cross over to the down line, on the right, to pass through the station and either into the north yard or, by using North Junction, to return to ex-LNWR metals. Beckett Street goods yard, to the left of the shed looks very busy, Clinker's Directory of Stations says that the power crane here could lift 12 tons. Notice the wooden 'portcullis' style structure over the goods shed entrance and the metal upright storage bike racks amongst the motley collection of structures by the loading dock. *Author's collection*

Below: **South of Oxford station, mid 1960s.** Looking north from the steps of Osney Mead footbridge shows one of the most interesting features of operations at Oxford station – locomotive changing. Pulling away smartly from the up platform onto the fast line is rebuilt 'Battle of Britain' class 4-6-0 No.34085 *501 Squadron* with an express for the Southern Region. On its right is Stanier Class Five 4-6-0 No. 45046 which displays Southern Region style headcode discs, waiting to take a train south. Many trains changed engines here as it was possible to work 'home and away' in one shift giving a good utilisation of crews and locos. Showing up well are the points for the down platform line from the through line and the former 'West Midland Sidings' on the left. The signal box has an outer brick skirt acquired in 1942 as a wartime precaution against bomb damage. *Cannings Photo Library*

Right, above: **Oxford station, 1956.** Oxford has always been a very busy station, but with limited accommodation for trains. Essentially, it consists of up and down platforms with bays on both sides at the north end. As can be seen in this view south from the down platform in a quiet moment, there were crossovers half way along both platform lines onto the through lines. While this allowed two short trains to use one platform at the same time, it blocked the through lines causing congestion. At this time passengers used a subway and there was better access from west Oxford onto the platforms. In 1958 620,000 tickets were issued from Oxford while in 1959 178 passenger and parcels trains as well as 150 freights passed through Oxford each day. *Stations UK*

Right, below: **Oxford station exterior, 1964.** Apart from enlargement in 1908, a time traveller would be able to recognise the station as Oxford. Certainly the cars would be novel but the wooden buildings and posters, albeit with different adverts, would not be new. Both up and down platforms were accessible from the Botley Road and a subway connected them. *R S Carpenter collection*

Below: **Oxford, 1904.** Like most railway companies the GWR's trains became longer and heavier over time. Consequently, bigger engines evolved to haul them. Hence 2-2-2s were superseded by 4-2-2 singles, with one of the latter seen here, then by 4-4-0s and latterly by 4-6-0s. The biggest and heaviest of these, the 'King' class, were not allowed south of Banbury, except in an emergency, probably due to weight restrictions on some bridges. An interesting sight here in April 1950, being tested for clearances, was the gas turbine engine, No.18000, weighing in at slightly more than a 'Castle' class engine and tender, which brought in six coaches from Paddington. *R S Carpenter collection*

Left, above: **Oxford station, undated**. Arriving at the up platform is an express hauled by one of the compound engines that the GWR experimented with in the early years of the twentieth century. This one is 4-4-2 No.102 *La France*. Better known for developing what they did well rather than 'new fangled ideas', the company wanted to see if compounds were worth the effort. So it bought three in kit form from France and assembled them at Swindon. These locos frequently hauled Paddington to Birmingham trains via Oxford and all three ended their days allocated here.
Author's collection

Left, below: **Oxford station, 24 October 1930**. As well as express trains to Worcester, Birmingham, Reading and London there were numerous local stopping train services radiating from here such as to Fairford, Banbury, Thame, and Didcot. In this picture 2-6-2T No.3915 complete with non-corridor coaches awaits passengers. Some local services used steam rail motors which served the specially built halts mentioned earlier; AEC diesel railcars were introduced in later years. *Author's collection*

Below: **Oxford station, 10 June 1933**. Scurrying along on the down through line is 'Duke' class 4-4-0 No.3256 *Guinevere* with a freight train. The water tower on the left and the imposing bracket signal were distinctive features at the end of the up platform. *L Hanson*

Right, above: **Oxford station, 24 September 1962.** Sorting sidings to the north and goods yards to the south meant a lot of transfer freights through the station. Performing such a humble role is '5700' class 0-6-0PT No.9653. The signals indicate that the next home signal could be 'on' and the driver should be prepared to stop. Many of the wooden buildings were probably original, dating from 1850, surviving until 1970. Prior to 1890 there was a Brunel style overall train shed across the four tracks. The crossovers show up well; the two ground signals allowing wrong direction workings. *P Harrod*

Right, below: **Oxford station, February 1954.** Heading south across the bridge carrying the line over the Sheepwater cut of the River Thames is WD 2-8-0 No.90485 with a class H freight, on the up through line. The array of signals was replaced by BR standard arms on a single gantry in November 1959. On the left are the wooden buildings that made up the engine shed. Note the schoolboys on the right wearing short trousers and gabardine coats while one has a school cap – contrast this with today's youngsters. *Author's collection*

Below: **Leaving Oxford, 1960.** Storming away past the signal gantry by the entrance to the engine shed is an express departing the down platform with 4-6-0 No.1013 *County of Dorset* in charge. The train is the 9.15am Margate to Birkenhead, also conveying through coaches from other seaside towns. Another south coast to northern city train was the famous 'Pines Express' which from 1962 to 1967 was routed through Oxford where it sometimes changed engines. Previously it travelled from Manchester through Birmingham, Gloucester and Bath, then over the Somerset & Dorset line to reach Bournemouth. *Author's collection*

Left, above: **London & North Western Railway, Oxford, 1938**. When coming from the city the terminus at Rewley Road was the first station passengers would encounter. It was also the first of the two adjacent stations to open, on 20 May 1851. Tracks went north from Oxford and then east to Bletchley where they met the LNWR main line. While there was an extensive goods yard the passenger accommodation was much more modest, consisting of two platform faces under a train shed. After the wartime connections put in between the two railway systems, the limited passenger services to Rewley Road were accommodated at the former GWR station, called 'Oxford General' from early BR days. The LMS experimental articulated diesel hydraulic set seen here was built as a three-car unit with a total of 162 seats. After languishing during the war it was used on electric lines in the Manchester area as a maintenance unit. *Lens of Sutton*

Left, below: **Oxford Engine Shed Signal Box, 1929**. Controlling movements at the north end of the station was a box similar to the one at the south end. The original box with this name was moved when the platforms were enlarged in 1908, to just south of the bridge over the river. The interior shows the large windows on the left which faced onto the running lines. Above is the track diagram. There were 97 levers in the box. The signalman would call out train movements to a booking boy who recorded them all in a train register. In 1942 the box became 'Station North' lasting until the power signal box took over in 1973.
Brunel University Railway Library, Mowat collection

Below: **Oxford shed, June 1914**. 2-2-2 No.165, on the allocation here, looks immaculate as it stands outside the shed in the sunshine, not long before withdrawal. No.165 was the last of the 'Cobham' class, also known as 'Sharpies'. The original GWR broad gauge shed, lasting until 1872, was at the north end of the up platform. On the other side of the main lines, the OWW built a small 'narrow gauge' wooden shed complete with turntable, which the GWR shared until the amalgamation of 1863. The OWW shed was gradually extended, a larger turntable added and a water tank of 24,000 gallons capacity put in the roof. Part of the problem with operations here was that the dead end coal line was adjacent to the access line and this restricted the shed's efficiency. Also only small tender engines could pass under the coaler so limiting the types of engines which could be serviced. *LCGB Ken Nunn collection*

Right: **Oxford shed, 1952**. Soon to be withdrawn ex-Midland & South Western Junction Railway 2-4-0 No.1335 waits its turn to be coaled. Wartime demands on traffic led to improved fuelling arrangements with the construction of a double sided coal stage in 1944. And with the wartime connection between the two adjacent railway companies, ex-LMS engines were frequent visitors for servicing. Consequently the ex-LMS shed closed in December 1950.

F W Shuttleworth

Above: **Oxford shed, 1950s**. A fine picture of how steam engines were serviced. 'Star' class 4-6-0 No.4061 *Glastonbury Abbey* is moving away after receiving several tubs of coal, with another tub ready for the next engine. To get the coal into the tubs, men shovelled it from wagons propelled up the steep ramp into the middle of the coal stage.   *Eric Sawford*

Right: **Oxford shed, 1963**. Looking across the main running lines shows the wooden shed in its final years, it closed early in January 1966. It remained a fairly modest four road affair even though it had 67 engines allocated in 1959. The shed was accessed directly from the down lines as well as the up through line to allow exchange of engines as quickly as possible. On the right is one of the two diesel shunters that were almost continuously on duty at Hinksey yard.

Joe Moss collection

The allocation at 81F Oxford in February 1954

0-4-2T	5	2-6-2T	7	4-4-0	1
0-6-0	1	4-6-0*	18	Railcar	3
0-6-0PT	15	2-6-0	4		
2-8-0	3	2-8-2T	4	**Total**	**61**

*Including 3 'Castles'

Above: **Oxford shed, undated**. With its tender full of coal 'Aberdare' class 2-6-0 No.2667 moves away from the shed for its next duty. Famous for plodding along on freight trains the class did sterling work for the GWR in times when receipts from goods were greater than from passengers. In the background is the wartime brick replacement North Box. *Author's collection*

Below: **Oxford North Junction, late 1940s**. A misty background makes St. Barnabas' church, on the left, ghost-like. The new coaling facility is on the right. Before World War 2 there was a marshalling yard north of the engine shed, where freight trains would be split and tripped to the Top yard for Beckett Street yard and other local sidings. The GWR practice for indicating signals for goods lines was, like the LNWR, to put a white hoop on the signal arm. Note the fine finials on top. LNER B17/4 class 4-6-0 No.2847 *Helmingham Hall* has the right of way to proceed along the down main towards Banbury. *Author's collection*

Above: **Oxford North Junction, circa 1955**. For the best part of 90 years, the connections between the parallel lines of the GWR and LNWR were via a loop just over the bridge from the station. Between North box on the GWR lines and the bridge over a cut in the River Thames was the site chosen to build a simple double junction between the two sets of lines, controlled by a new GWR signal box. It was often referred to as 'Wartime Direct Junction'. Heading a train to Cambridge is LNER D16/3 class 4-4-0 No. 62618. Waiting in the up goods loop is a freight train with an interesting assortment of wagons and types of loads. Note the water column, fed by the tower hiding the signal box. Telegraph poles rule.   *Author's collection*

Below: **Oxford North Junction, 23 May 1954**. This fine track level picture has been included as it shows several of the wartime alterations here. The North sidings were converted into loops as part of the improvements and were later used as carriage sidings, with Hinksey yards taking over all the freight operations. In the midst of all the GWR type signals is a lone upper quadrant. As the Western Region was the only one that operated lower quadrant signals, BR wanted to harmonise things, so it erected various types of signals here and at Portishead for assessment purposes. The train arriving from Bletchley has a BR Standard 2-6-4T, believed to be No.80042, less than two years old.

Mile Post 92¹/₂ Picture Library, A W V Mace collection

Wolvercot to King's Sutton

Above: **Wolvercot, circa 1960**. One of the crack expresses passing here was the morning train from Hereford and Worcester to London. Worcester shed had a fleet of 'Castle' class 4-6-0s for duties such as this – always immaculately turned out too. Having come off the OWW line from Worcester about 33 chains away, No.5032 *Usk Castle* has shut off steam as it prepares for the stop at Oxford station's up platform, some two and a half miles south. Note the imposing telegraph pole between the down main and down loop on the left. On the right is the LNWR line to Bicester and Bletchley. The up and down loops and associated signal box were 1941 additions to the system. *Author's collection*

Below: **Wolvercot, 1921**. Approaching Oxford is an up express with 'Flower' class 4-4-0 No.4158 *Petunia*. On the right is another glimpse of the LNWR line to Bletchley. To the right of the train is an up loop which was laid from Wolvercot Junction to Oxford station in 1900; it took wartime conditions to repeat the process on the down side. *LGRP*

Right, above: **Wolvercot sidings, circa 1907**. This was a loop on the down side. Traditionally, trailing access was by a single slip from the up main and by a point onto the down main. In June 1900, the GWR built an up loop past here, rebuilding the signal box, which is the one in this view, Wolvercot Siding. There was also a gated public footpath to Port Meadow which crossed the lines. A down loop was added to the left from 1942.

Lens of Sutton

Right, below: **Wolvercot Platform**. To serve passengers in North Oxford, both railway companies constructed wooden platforms made from railway sleepers. The GWR structure seen here was open from 1 February 1908 until 1 January 1918. It was adjacent to the canal with foot access only from the surrounding area. The LNWR had two halts – one at Port Meadow (originally called Summertown Halt) and one at Wolvercote (*sic*), open from 20 October 1905 until 25 October 1926, with a temporary closure from 1 January 1917 until 5 May 1919.

Lens Of Sutton

Below: **Wolvercot, 13 June 1914**. Having left Blenheim at 2.50pm, steam railmotor No.74, with a gas tank wagon in tow, nears Wolvercot Platform and, after pausing, will carry on into Oxford station. The railmotors did not perform too well when required to haul an extra carriage as the service became popular, so the GWR developed the more familiar push-pull trains to take over this work.

LCGB, Ken Nunn collection

Line to Worcester

Left, above: **Wolvercot Junction.** Arriving from the west is 'The Cathedrals Express' from Hereford and Worcester. Hauling it is No.7034 *Ince Castle.* The main line, towards Banbury, heads north, curving away to the right. The line on the extreme right is the up goods, accessible from both the Worcester and Banbury directions. *David Lawrence*

Left, below: **Yarnton signal box, 1960.** In 1854 the LNWR built a connection from its Bletchley line, which crossed over the Banbury line and joined the Worcester line here. It was able to offer a service from Euston to Worcester by this means. Also a simple curve was constructed to create a triangle on its own metals so that trains could also run into its Oxford station from Worcester. While the latter connection was short-lived and the Euston service withered too, the connection from here to Bletchley was extensively used in World War 2 as a diversionary line for many freight trains, to increase capacity and reduce the chances of bomb damage. A wartime marshalling yard was built south of Yarnton station for exchange of traffic on the various routes. *Lens of Sutton*

Below: **Yarnton station, 7 June 1960.** A branch line to Witney opened from here in 1861; extension to Cheltenham was planned but only got as far as Fairford in 1873, with the rest of the scheme being abandoned. To coincide with the opening of the Witney line the West Midland Railway opened a station here on 14 November 1861 which remained in operation until 18 June 1962. Behind the photographer is the line to Oxford and the LNWR connection to Bletchley. On the up main line is a freight from Worcester hauled by 4-6-0 No.6924 *Grantley Hall.* The steel bracket signal has the shorter post for the branch and the taller post for the down main line. *Millbrook House Ltd*

Above: **Kidlington, 1962.** Opened as Langford Lane in 1855, quickly changing its name to Woodstock Road by July that year, the station became 'Kidlington for Blenheim' from 19 May 1890, then latterly 'Kidlington change for Blenheim & Woodstock' – the palace first and village second! Looking south towards Oxford from the adjacent road bridge, rebuilt in 1936, shows the main lines well spaced out, having been constructed to accommodate the broad gauge. The goods shed to the right shows similar evidence; the other siding used to serve a Harris's bacon factory. During the 1940s the footbridge's canopy was removed. On the platforms were facilities for ladies on the up and gentlemen on the down! A bay for Blenheim trains, with a small loading dock at its end, is to the right of the down platform. *P J Garland, R S Carpenter collection*

Below: **Kidlington, 1962.** A typical GWR signal box is on the up side and there is still some unrecovered rail which was part of an up loop. The offset bracket signal was to improve sighting due to the curve in the track. Going under the road bridge is the line leading to the Blenheim branch, it paralleled the main lines for over a mile before turning west. The station closed on 2 November 1964, some ten years after the branch. *P J Garland, R S Carpenter collection*

Branch to Blenheim

Left, above: **Shipton-On-Cherwell, 1954**. The only intermediate station on the just over three and a half miles-long branch was opened on 1 April 1929 where the line crossed the A423. The halt, of standard sleeper construction, and with lights, was on the north side of the line with access by a gravel track from the public road. *Stations UK*

Left, below: **Blenheim & Woodstock, 1949**. The branch was opened on 19 May 1890 by the Woodstock Railway, built by the Duke of Marlborough, and was operated by the GWR. It was worth the investment with over 20,000 passengers travelling in its early days. In 1910 there were up to ten trains a day. From 1929, most were of the push-pull type. Pannier tank 0-6-0PT No.5413, making a change from the more usual 0-4-2T, has arrived with auto trailer W58. *Joe Moss collection*

Below: **Blenheim & Woodstock, exterior, 1954**. Looking across the main A34 Oxford to Stratford road shows the brick 'L' shaped buildings with the platform beyond. With increasing road competition, passenger numbers dropped after the war, and by 1952 it was less than 9,000. The timetable showed eight trains each way on weekdays though only one went through to Oxford with two from Oxford to Blenheim. Most of the trains which terminated at Kidlington were not at times that allowed decent connections on the main line. Needless to say the line soon closed, on 1 March 1954. Pullen's glove factory was a good customer of the line, right up to closure.
Mile Post 92¹/₂ Picture Library, A W V Mace collection

Above: **Bletchington, 1925**. Looking south towards Oxford shows the plant of the Oxford & Shipton Cement Works in the distance. From November 1927 this was connected by a series of loops on the down side. Prior to 1925 the signal box was on the down platform but was moved behind the platform with the extension and remodelling of the down loop and the down refuge siding. Due to the curvature of the line the up home signals are on a post adjacent to the signal box, next to the bracket signal for the down lines.　　　　*Brunel University, Mowat collection*

Below: **Bletchington, 1963**. Just before the line crosses the Oxford Canal and the River Cherwell, a station called Woodstock was opened by the Oxford & Rugby Railway on 2 September 1850. Its name changed to Woodstock Road in May 1851, then to Kirtlington in July 1855, before settling on Bletchington from 11 August 1890. At opening, the single broad gauge line on the down side carried the four daily trains each way. Doubling, and adding the 'narrow' line, was carried out in time for the start of Oxford to Birmingham services in 1852. Looking north shows the limited freight facilities, including the unusual looking half shed. The station eventually closed on 2 November 1964.

Stations UK

Above: **Tackley Halt, 1958**. A small halt was opened on 6 April 1931, approximately a mile and a half north of Bletchington and just under two and a half miles south of Heyford. Looking towards Banbury shows well the use of sleepers for such halts and the comparative luxury of the up and down shelters. *Stations UK*

Left, above: **Heyford**. This was the site of a small station opened by the Oxford & Rugby Railway on 2 September 1850. There were substantial stone buildings on both platforms with a signal box on the down side. This view south shows the connection of the down siding trailing into the main line; a similar arrangement also existed on the other side. *Lens of Sutton*

Left, below: **Fritwell & Somerton, circa 1930**. While the others at opening in 1850 had a single line, here it was double track from 1852. Interestingly, the station's facilities were wooden buildings whereas most of the stations along the line are of stone or brick. As often happened, there were name changes, originally Somerton in 1855, becoming Somerton (Oxon) on 2 July 1906, then Fritwell & Somerton on 1 July 1907 up to closure on 2 November 1964. Just north of the station was a loop on the up side which looked after the area's freight needs with a loading dock and small shed. The signal box can be made out on the down side. *Brunel University, Mowat collection*

Above: **Aynho, 1954**. This was one of the three stations on the line when the Oxford & Rugby Railway opened on 2 September 1850. The suffix 'for Deddington' was added soon after. The broad gauge legacy still lingers on here. Not only are the pair of running lines further apart than is necessary for 'narrow' gauge trains but also the goods shed wagon entrance in the rear was built to accommodate the wider gauge. If this view had been taken before the 1910 construction of the Princes Risborough cut-off then the single line girder bridge, spanning the lines in the distance, would not have been visible. This bridge takes the down London line from the Souldern viaduct over the Oxford tracks. *Stations UK*

Right, above: **Aynho, 1963**. Note the influence of Brunel in the all round awning on the station buildings and the symmetrical appearance of the adjacent road overbridge in this view towards Oxford. Before its demolition, the up shelter at Stonehouse in Gloucestershire was very similar in design to the up shelter here, apart from slightly different stone. On either side of the station were loops, the up side dating from 1912 and the down side three years later. *Stations UK*

Right, below: **Aynho goods yard, 1962**. The crane here had a capacity of two tons. There was, for a rural station, a reasonable goods yard. Accessed by means of a trailing slip across the main lines, it consisted of a shed, cattle dock and three sidings. As with various other stations on the route, the passenger service ceased from 2 November 1964. *R K Blencowe collection*

Above, and left, above: **Aynho Park, 1963**. This new line reduced the distance between London and Birmingham by enough for the company to introduce two hour timings between the two cities, condemning Oxford to secondary line status. Opened with the London extension in 1910, for goods on 4 April and passengers on 1 July was Aynho Park which had a road level Booking Office, seen in 1962, with ramps to the platforms. These were of sleeper construction with wooden buildings on each side. Both up and down London lines had loops which only lasted until 1917. Oddly, for all the emphasis on high speed running, the down junction here is still subject to a 40 mph speed restriction. Like vicars of rural parishes, there was one station master for both stations in the village – this one closed on 7 January 1963. *P J Garland, R S Carpenter collection; Lens of Sutton*

Left, below: **Aynho Junction, line to London, 1960**. About a mile and a half south of King's Sutton station was the junction for the GWR's 'Direct' line to London. This picture was taken from the window of a down train, having just passed over the Oxford lines on the single girder bridge in the background. It will now have to wait at Aynho Junction while an express bound for Banbury and the Eastern Region passes along the down main line. At Banbury the 'Hall' class loco seen in this picture will be exchanged for an ex-LNER engine for the train's journey to Sheffield. The single up line passes across the picture behind the fine signal post.

Mile Post 92$^{1}/_{2}$ Picture Library, A W V Mace collection

Right: **Aynho Junction, 1962**. 2-6-2T No.4176 joins the line from Oxford with a load of limestone, being transported in iron ore hoppers from Ardley quarry to the cement works at Greaves Siding.   *M Mensing*

Below: **King's Sutton water troughs, 17 April 1954**. Ignoring the troughs, conveniently adjacent to the River Cherwell, is an auto-train from Banbury on its way to Princes Risborough. The engine hauling the single trailer is 1400 class 0-4-2T No.1411. On the return journey the driver will control the propelling loco from a special compartment at the front of the coach. To improve timings and save waits at stations the GWR introduced water troughs on flat, roughly straight, stretches of line so that engines could fill up on the move.

T E Williams

Above, left: **King's Sutton Junction**. This gives an excellent view of the junction at King's Sutton – the main line in the centre, with the branch to Adderbury, Chipping Norton, Kingham and Cheltenham curving off to the right. *M Hale*

Above, right: **King's Sutton**. Curved frame 'Badminton' class 4-4-0 No.4112 *Oxford* hurries through the station with a Newcastle to Bournemouth train which includes London & South Western and Great Central Railway stock.
R M Casserley collection

Left: **King's Sutton signal box interior, 1955**. This was the second box to bear the name. The first was close to the south end of the down platform. With the extra traffic resulting from the doubling of the line towards Cheltenham from 1906, it was decided to move the box adjacent to the junction. To give a clear view of all lines it was rebuilt on the up side with the up loop passing behind it. This depicts a signalman's work place: the windows looking out onto the junction, a block shelf with instruments in front and the frame below. The bells and dials of the instruments were the official way of communicating with the boxes on either side – Aynho Junction to the south and Astrop Sidings in the down direction. By releasing the catch on the lever, it could be moved to operate the points and signals under the box's control. The box closed in April 1971; the branch had stayed open only as far as Adderbury up to April 1970, after which a short section at King's Sutton was retained as a siding until the box's closure. *Signalling Record Society, Scrimgeour collection*

Above: **King's Sutton, early 1960s.** Over twenty years after the line first saw trains a station was opened here on 2 August 1872 by the GWR. In 1909 the platforms were extended by 100 feet and, to make it safe to cross the line, due to the impending arrival of 'direct' London trains, a footbridge was built. The goods yard was enlarged by the addition of two new sidings with trailing connections on the up side, on the left. Although the station is still open in this picture it was downgraded to the status of 'Halt' from 1 November 1964, until 6 May 1968. While the delightful down side shelter escaped demolition, the fine main building on the up side with its distinctive ornate chimneys didn't.
Lens of Sutton

Line to Cheltenham via Kingham

Below: **Adderbury, circa 1950.** Arriving from Banbury is 0-6-0PT No.5404. Note the station's facilities are all at one end of both platforms, which had been lengthened in 1906. The Banbury & Cheltenham Direct line, opened in 1887, left the main line just south of King's Sutton station, before crossing the ever present River Cherwell and the Oxford Canal. Built as a single line, it was doubled to here in 1906. The first part of the line was rich in iron ore which went to South Wales or the Midlands. Most passenger services were to Chipping Norton Junction (renamed Kingham in 1909) where trains to Cheltenham could be caught. In 1906, along with the improvements mentioned above, the GWR built an avoiding line at Chipping Norton Junction to obviate reversal for through workings such as the famous 'Ports to Ports ' train which ran over the route until the outbreak of World War 2. The station closed on 4 July 1951.
Author's collection

Banbury

Above: **Near Astrop Sidings, 6 March 1965**. A cross-country express on its way to Oxford along the up fast line leaves the melting snow at Banbury. The train came from York via the ex-Great Central line through Leicester and is destined for Bournemouth, the engine being 'Jubilee' class 4-6-0 No.45694 *Bellerophon*. It will probably be changed at Oxford for a Southern Region engine. The signal box near here originally controlled access to loops for a long since closed adjacent quarry and, from 1908, the four lines to Banbury South box. On the left is the engine shed. A footnote from the war – a German air raid scored a direct hit on the gasometer in 1941. *R K Blencowe collection*

Below: **Banbury shed, 24 May 1959**. It was not until October 1908, preceding the opening of the cut-off to London and after the link to the Great Central main line, that the GWR built a suitably large engine shed here – four roads complete with a 55' turntable south of the station. Like Oxford it was extended as part of wartime improvements, in 1944. The new layout was designed to reduce the time engines spent on shed so increasing their availability. Amongst other things this involved the addition of the four roads to the left to increase capacity. The proposed further extension of part brick and cladding was never built, but a new corrugated lifting shop was, seen on the left. Two ash shelters were also added. *R K Blencowe collection*

The allocation at 84C Banbury in February 1954

0-6-0	7	2-6-2T	3	4-6-0	15
2-8-0	19	0-6-0PT	16	2-6-0	5
				Total	**65**

Banbury shed. In its heyday, locally based 'Bulldog' class 4-4-0 No.3399 *Ottawa* (*right, above*) would have been used for express passenger duties, but by the 1930s when this picture was taken, the loco was normally diagrammed on more mundane work – it was one of five of the class allocated here. In the view taken on 29 March 1936 (*right, below*) 'Mogul' No.4361, also a Banbury engine, shares the shed with LNER 'Ivatt Atlantic' 4-4-2 No.4434, which had probably arrived via the Great Central line from the East Midlands; the class worked the night mails train as far as Swindon. No. 4361 was useful on any duty from humble pick-up freights to express work such as the Newcastle-South Wales 'Ports-to-Ports' train which traversed the cross-country line threading over the Cotswolds between Banbury and Cheltenham. In 1934, Banbury was home to fifteen Churchward 2-6-0s. Wartime alterations at the shed in 1944 included the extension of the coaling stage to become double-sided, new ash shelter and lifting shop. On 10 December 1965, 'Britannia' Pacific No.70053 (*below*), devoid of its name *Moray Firth*, has been turned and had its tender filled. The loco will now proceed to be watered then stabled in one of the shed roads. From September 1965 Banbury had eight 'Britannias' allocated, though their work was concentrated on the Great Central line out of London Marylebone. But they all moved away to Carlisle during January 1966. Following regional boundary changes, Banbury shed became part of the London Midland Region in September 1963, coded 2D, having been 84C previously in the BR era and BAN in GWR days. The shed closed to steam in October 1966.   *Photomatic; L Hanson; Cox*

Left, above: **Arriving at Banbury, 17 February 1962**. Passing the engine shed, to the right, and the gasometer, to the left, is a special, 1Z30, hauled by 4-6-0 No.7014 *Caerhays Castle*. The signal post on the right gave direction to engines leaving the shed: proceed to the goods shed (behind the South box); to the station; or to the up side; or to the marshalling yard. The engine is passing over the points where the down goods joins the down main. *S V Blencowe collection*

Left, below: **Leaving Banbury, 16 April 1961**. The signalman in South box has set the road on the fine bracket signal for the up fast line as 'King' class 4-6-0 No.6014 *King Henry VII* gets away with express A28. The other signals on the bracket are left, to the engine shed, and, right, to the up slow line. Although 'Kings' were the most powerful of the GWR's locomotives, due to their weight they were normally prohibited south of here along the original main line. The doubling of the exhaust ports in the chimney improved their performance. In early 1956 problems with their front bogies led to them being temporarily withdrawn and a few ex-LMS Stanier 'Pacifics' including Nos.46207, 46210 and 46254 were drafted in to work some turns, including trains known to railwaymen for years as the 'Zulu' – the 9.10am London Paddington to Wolverhampton and Birkenhead and 11.40am from Birkenhead (2.35pm ex-Wolverhampton) to London. *A Delicata*

Below: **Banbury, 7 March 1966**. Using the full potential of the new station is a train about to enter platform 1 on the down loop line; the South signal box can be seen above the coaches. On the right is the 'new' goods shed, the original wooden one was rebuilt in brick – just in time for it to be reduced to a heap of bricks by an air raid in 1940. This is now the site of the car park. Hauling the Bournemouth West to York is Class Five 4-6-0 No.45264. After the stop here, it will proceed along the former GCR main line towards Sheffield. By this time this former GWR heartland had passed to LMR jurisdiction, something not looked upon with any joy by diehard GWR men! *R J Buckley, Initial Photographics*

Right, above: **Banbury station exterior, circa 1900**. While the GWR broad gauge station opened on 2 September 1850, the LNWR station at Merton Street commenced operations in May that year. Thus the town, population around 8,500, had two termini stations, both looking temporary, being constructed of wood. The Bradshaw timetable of the day called the GWR station 'Bridge Street'. Looking not a lot different fifty years or so after opening by the broad gauge Oxford & Rugby Railway, its two platforms had a Brunel style wooden train shed to provide some protection for passengers. The down platform was 350' long, a full 100' longer than the up platform. From 1883 a footbridge inside the train shed connected the platforms. To the left of the entrance/booking hall is a small refreshment room that would soon be replaced by a brick structure.	*Newton collection*

Right, below: **Banbury station, 27 May 1933**. The extent of the 1903 rebuilding of the station to provide five platform faces can be seen. The view is from the extended up main platform 1 and the similar extension to the down platform 3 can be seen through the train shed. The goods shed prevented further extension of the down platform. At the northern end were platforms 2, down side, and 5, up side, while to the right platform 4 is occupied by a clerestory coach and a gas tank wagon, used to refill the containers in auto coaches. The station name boards on the left are interesting – the closest one simply has the town's name on it, while the furthest says 'Change here for the Banbury and Cheltenham line'.	*Mowat collection*

Below: **Banbury, April 1956**. It was rather obvious that the ancient train shed, having suffered the elements and engine exhausts for a century was in need of replacement, so it probably did not need much help to come down in 1952. The footbridge was covered over and awnings put over the main platforms. The opportunity has been taken to generally tidy up the station while the name boards are developing a history of their own – one proclaims that, in the BR era, it is now 'Banbury General' and has swapped places with another board that states 'Change here for the Eastern Region'.	*Rail Archive Stephenson*

Above: **Banbury**. Construction in 1900 of a branch from the Great Central Railway's Woodford & Hinton station to Banbury Junction, about a mile north of the station, enabled much cross-country working to be undertaken. LNER B1 4-6-0 No.5196 – one of only two members of this ex-GCR class – has arrived at the up main platform with a train for the south. It is likely that an engine change will not take place until the train arrives at Oxford. No.5196 and its sister No.5195 were renumbered 1480 and 1479 in 1946 but were both withdrawn from service in 1947 –- they should not be confused with the much more common LNER Thompson B1 class. *R Blencowe collection*

Below: **Banbury, 1957**. Although sanctioned in 1937, the station rebuilding was delayed by the outbreak of war in 1939. The station simply had to be moved to the west by about fifteen feet then a down through line could be put in. Temporary passenger access was by the big footbridge while the new station rises in the background. At the head of three LNER coaches is abundant power in the form of V2 2-6-2 No.60812 in the bay platform 5 at the northern end of the up platform. Normally the four daily trains shuttling between the two main lines were hauled by GCR, later, LNER engines. They would run into the station, use the run-round facilities, then move the stock and wait in the bay on the other side of the main line, platform 2. *Stations UK*

Above: **Banbury, 1950**. The southern up bay, platform 4, was the starting place for trains to Princes Risborough, along the cut off, and the line to Cheltenham. Members of the 1400 class 0-4-2T were common engines on these auto trains, although pannier tanks were used too. The loco's water tank is being filled from the swan neck column while the fireman chats to an eager group of young rail enthusiasts. In the background is the single road 1889 shed that was built after the opening of the 'Direct' line to Cheltenham in 1887 and which sufficed until 1908. By the time of this picture it was used to clean and repair auto coaches and for stabling the auto engine. *Lens of Sutton collection*

Right, above: **Banbury, 1958**. Life goes on amidst the construction work. The contractors, Marples, built reinforced concrete supports and put awnings on them. 0-6-0PT No.5420 waits at the head of a local stopping train. *S V Blencowe collection*

Right, below: **Banbury, 30 July 1960**. The original pre-war plan was for two island platforms with a bay at the departure end of each, not unlike the finished article. With the time almost 4 o'clock the 3.30pm from Oxford prepares to leave for Birmingham with 2-6-0 No.6349 in charge. This train was a diesel multiple unit from Monday to Friday, and engine and coaches on Saturday. It was a semi-fast, stopping only at Banbury, Leamington Spa and Warwick, due into Birmingham Snow Hill at 5.6pm, the steam timing being nine minutes slower than the DMU. *R J Buckley, Initial Photographics*

Above: **Banbury, exterior and interior, 1958.** What a contrast to the previous external view. All passengers now had to go up stairs as these new buildings were west of the new through line. It needs to be remembered that even though the war was well over by this time, the hangover from days of rationing was still in people's minds and the boom years of the 1960s had yet to happen. This building symbolised the start of a new era. Compared to earlier views north this clean and elegant station with its sweeping platforms was greatly admired. It broke with tradition having the refreshment rooms on the wide footbridge above the main lines. *British Railways*

Below: **Ex-LNWR station, Banbury, 18 March 1961.** This was the first railway to arrive in the town with a single line branch from the LNWR main line at Bletchley. The company built a wooden terminal station accessed from Merton Street, probably intending it to be a temporary affair. It opened in May 1850, a few months before the GWR. Cattle traffic was a substantial part of the revenue for railway companies here – not surprising as it was a very agricultural area with Banbury for years hosting the largest livestock market in Europe. *F A Blencowe*

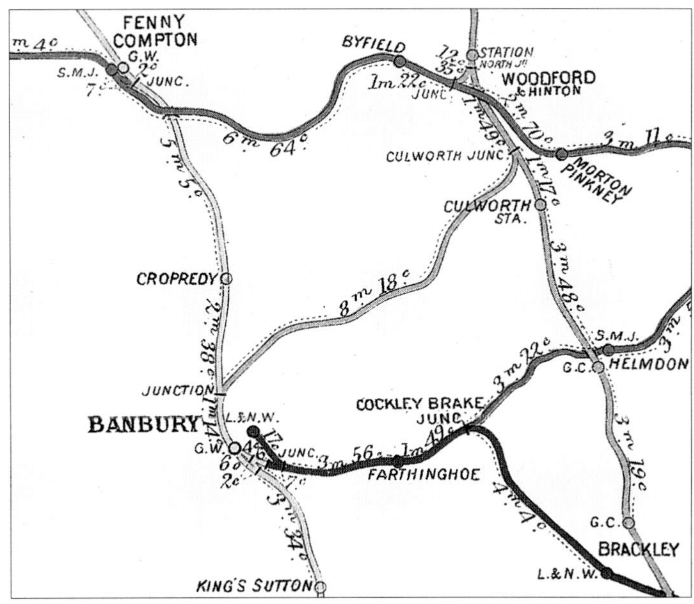

Above: **Banbury, 1963**. A class D, partially fitted, freight train passes through the station on the down loop line, which was put in during the rebuild. The signalman from the North box has lowered the arm on the left of the bracket signal to indicate to the driver that he can proceed behind the box and north towards Banbury Junction. The engine is No.2822, one of the sixty year old class of 2-8-0s designed for heavy freight traffic by G J Churchward.

B W L Brooksbank, Initial Photographics

Below: **Banbury yard, 13 July 1963**. Standing next to the down main line looking towards Leamington shows North Signal box and the connection of the down through line to the down goods emerging behind it. On the extreme right is a ubiquitous BR 350hp diesel shunter, with the southern ends of the loops from the hump yard next to it. In the centre is the siding used by the station pilot involved in adding and removing carriages, vans and wagons from a variety of trains. *F A Blencowe*

Banbury yard, May 1931. At this date this rural Oxfordshire town had a population of 14,000. Its freight services were looked after by a shed and loops on the down side just before the station and cattle facilities opposite the station on the up side. Five extra sidings were added north of the station on the up side in 1884, presumably in preparation for the 'Direct' line to Cheltenham which opened three years later. These were enlarged to eleven and it was from these 'North End Sidings' that southbound services departed. The GC connection resulted in nine dead end sidings on the down side and seven similar sidings on the up side along the branch. In 1903, both up and down loops were put in from north of the station to Banbury Junction. Congestion continued with the general growth of traffic and so the North End Sidings were replaced by a new hump yard in 1931. Between the GCR junction and the hump were four reception loops. Next came the 1 in 240 ramp up to the top of the hump – from where this official picture was taken – which fed nineteen loops. The capacity of the yard was put at 1,396 wagons and soon after opening something like 1,700 wagons passed over the hump in 24 hours. *Oxfordshire County Council Photographic Archive; R Tourret collection*

Above: **Banbury yard, 5 March 1959**. The time is just after 8.30am and there is plenty of activity at the southern end of the yard with two freight trains. First to depart would be the train on the left, the 8.40am to Westbury via Oxford with No.5982 *Harrington Hall* while on the right is the 9am for Old Oak Common via Princes Risborough behind Banbury's own 2-8-0 No.2816. Both trains would probably have been assembled during the night. To the right were connections to the set of seven dead end sidings for local traffic. On the left is a siding which rises up towards the buffer stop. Brake vans were stored there, with their brakes screwed down, and these were attached to the ends of trains as and when needed by gravity. *Author's collection*

Below: **Banbury Junction, 29 June 1961**. Passing along the down main line with a fitted van train is double chimney 4-6-0 No.4074 *Caldicot Castle*. To the right is a loop that was used as a reception for the down sidings – the end of one can be seen to the right, on the other side of the down goods line. To the left of the train are the up main lines with the four original yard reception lines, which had been enlarged to six, beyond them. In the distance is the hump and its loops with the controlling signal box. *S V Blencowe*

Line to Great Central Railway

Above: **Banbury Junction, October 1948.** Signalled to proceed onto the up goods line is a parcels train from the north hauled by an unidentifiable, grimy, 'Hall' class 4-6-0. The other two arms on the bracket signal were for the up main, on the left, and the route to the reception sidings, on the right. The GC up yard shows up well as does the catch point and protecting signal for shunting on the down GC line.   *Millbrook House Ltd*

Left, above: **Banbury Junction, October 1948.** Facing north sees War Department 2-8-0 No.77318 (later BR No.90007) coming along the line from Woodford Halse, no doubt with its characteristic clanking. It is signalled to pass into one of the reception sidings by the small signal. Behind the engine are the up sidings for the GC line with the signals having hoops on them to indicate that they are for goods lines only, not the main line. Above the loco steam the elevated up signal for the main line can just be made out.
Millbrook House Ltd

Left, below: **Woodford Halse, 30 July 1960.** Along the 11 mile Banbury-Woodford Halse connection just four trains served the two intermediate halts, Charcombe (or Chalcombe as some would spell it) and Eydon in 1949, so local passenger traffic was marginal and its real value was for cross-country freight and passenger trains. One such, the 12.13pm Ramsgate to Derby Friargate, is seen entering Woodford Halse station, previously called Woodford & Hinton. In charge, probably since Oxford, is Class Five 4-6-0 No.45186 based at Saltley shed, 21A. With its connections to the GC lines, to the north, and routes to the south coast, Banbury was somewhat of a crossroads – seaside towns like Southampton, Deal and Bournemouth all had through coaches via Banbury to Newcastle, Glasgow and Birkenhead. Conversely York, Wolverhampton and Birkenhead dispatched coaches to Margate, Weymouth, Bournemouth and Swindon. These workings were a challenge to the railway system in regards to connections and efficient timekeeping, while giving a sense of cohesiveness to the traveller.
R J Buckley, Initial Photographics

Banbury's capacity for dealing with freight can be gauged by this list of sidings shown in the 1960 *Sectional Appendix to the Working Time Table*. In 1955/56 five shunting engines worked seven days a week – one at Banbury Hump, Junction end; one at Banbury Hump and Local Yards; one at Banbury General South End; two at Banbury Junction.

BANBURY GENERAL – holding capacity 486 wagons
11 Down Sidings – South End – including private siding traffic for Midland Tar Distillers
6 Up Sidings – South End – including Live Stock Traffic and Auto Cars for cleaning etc.

BANBURY HUMP YARD – holding capacity 1943 wagons plus 10 brake vans
6 Reception Sidings
20 Hump Sidings
1 Brake Van Siding (for 10 brake vans)
7 Local Yard Sidings
6 Cripple and Storage Sidings

BANBURY JUNCTION – holding capacity 1050 wagons
6 Down Side Front Yard Sidings
8 Down Side Back Yard Sidings
8 Up Side Storage Sidings – including shunting spur
5 Grange Private Sidings – up side of line at Banbury Junction, connecting from No.6 Hump Reception Siding, holding capacity 40 wagons, engine and van.

Banbury to Hatton Junctions

Below: **Ironstone branch, Wroxton, 16 June 1958**. Just half a mile north from Banbury Junction was the interchange with the Oxfordshire Ironstone Company's branch to Wroxton Quarries. The ironstone workings were an important source of traffic for the GWR and BR. The company was established in 1917, and built four 1200' sidings on the down side holding 60 wagons. The work was paid for by Ministry of Munitions and carried out by German POWs. 81,346 tons was mined in 1919, going up to 1.75 million tons in 1956. Trains of iron ore went north from the sidings and at Hatton Junction some went south to South Wales and others to the Bilston Works of Stewarts & Lloyds. Much of the branch was double track. The locomotive depicted on a train of dumpcars, Peckett 0-4-0ST *Maud*, was new here in 1938. Motive power was in the form of 0-4-0ST, 0-6-0ST, 0-6-0T and a lone Sentinel 4-wheeled geared loco; sometimes there were no fewer than nine engines working each day. The smaller engines were used at the face of the opencast quarries, the lines being moved to keep pace with the excavations. The use of diesels started in the early 1960s. It is estimated that when quarrying finished in 1971 something like 33 million tons of ore had been removed. The quarries received a Royal visit from the Duke of Edinburgh on 6 November 1957. *H C Casserley; R M Casserley*

Right: **Cropredy, early 1960s**. The station was opened by the Oxford & Rugby Railway on 1 October 1852, and closed by BR on 17 September 1956. Looking south towards Banbury shows the junction of the down goods loop with the down main adjacent to the signal box. This loop stretched all the way from Banbury. On the up side, a short loop accessed by a trailing slip led to two goods sidings. The Oxford Canal had a wharf at nearby Fenny Compton before heading off to meet the Grand Union Canal at Napton Junction. *Lens of Sutton*

Left, above: **Fenny Compton, 15 March 1952**. This featured in two company's proposals, as part of the 1845 Oxford & Rugby Railway and the 1846 Birmingham & Oxford Junction Railways' Acts. It was actually opened on 1 October 1852 by the GWR with up and down platforms adjacent to a level crossing. South of these was a very small goods yard on the down side. However, when the line from Bedford to Stratford-upon-Avon was opened its platforms were adjacent to the GWR allowing passenger exchange. But this left the GWR goods yard sandwiched between two sets of running lines. When business increased the GWR down platform was rebuilt north of the level crossing resulting in staggered platforms. From late 1902 a goods shed was added to the goods yard. 4-6-0 No.6924 *Grantley Hall* is passing the up platform and is about to traverse the level crossing ready to stop at the down platform on a Banbury – Leamington service, consisting of a single auto-coach – somewhat overwhelmed by the motive power! *H C Casserley*

Left, below: **Fenny Compton, early 1960s**. While from opening of the East & West Junction Railway there was a probably a connection between the two sets of goods facilities it was not until 1960 that the lines were remodelled to allow through running in both directions. This view towards Leamington shows the remains of the S&MJR platform – the one with the train featured below – on the left. The other platform has been removed and a new signal box controls the new signals. On the right is the up main line platform which closed on 2 November 1964. The S&MJR line is still open for 3½ miles as far as the military base at Burton Dassett, also known as Kineton. *Lens of Sutton*

Below: **Fenny Compton, circa 1939**. The East & West Junction Railway's line east to Bedford and west to Stratford-upon-Avon passed over the GWR Oxford to Birmingham route here. Becoming the Stratford-upon-Avon & Midland Junction Railway in 1909, its station was named Fenny Compton West for its brief BR existence, opening on 1 June 1871, closed 1 August 1877, reopening on 22 February 1885, before closing for ever on 7 April 1952. Around the date of this picture there were three daily passenger trains from Stratford to Blisworth, on the ex-LNWR main line between Rugby and London Euston. An ageing Johnson Midland 3F 0-6-0 No.3529 is at the station. On the opposite platform is the signal box, complete with fire buckets. *Stations UK*

Right, above: **Greaves Siding, 2 April 1983**. Access to a cement works was controlled by this box. Typically, there was a trailing slip from the up main line with a connection to the down main line. One of the sidings was extended towards Southam Road station to become a down goods loop from 27 July 1907. *J G S Smith*

Right, below: **Southam Road & Harbury, circa 1955**. This station was another opened by the Birmingham & Oxford Junction on 1 October 1852. Viewed from the down platform, an unidentified 'Hall' class 4-6-0 heads a southbound express through the station. Another train waits in the up refuge siding judging by the plume of smoke above the second carriage and the wagons visible beyond the last coach. Note the connections from the main lines to the goods yard on the left, consisting of a loading dock, goods shed and two sidings. The station was another closing on 2 November 1964; one nameboard is now in Kidderminster Railway Museum. *Joe Moss collection*

Below: **Harbury cutting & tunnel, 24 July 1943**. Leamington Spa is actually at the bottom of a dip in the land. Consequently, the line north from Southam Road & Harbury, six miles away, is at a falling gradient of 1 in 187. To keep to this gradient a deep cutting was necessary, at one point being 110' deep. Across the area is a narrow ridge of land passing east to west. The railway decided to pierce the ridge with a 73 yard tunnel instead of going over it and so kept the gradients manageable. The access road to Bull Ring Farm provided the vantage point for this view of an iron ore train drifting downhill from the tunnel towards Leamington Spa. Up trains were often banked to enable them to climb the gradient and until 1920 there was a crossover to allow banking locos to return to Leamington. Hauling the train is a wartime American import doing sterling service before being shipped off to the continent. It is S160 class 2-8-0 No.2318. Taking pictures in wartime was a risky business hence their scarcity.
V R Webster collection, Kidderminster Railway Museum

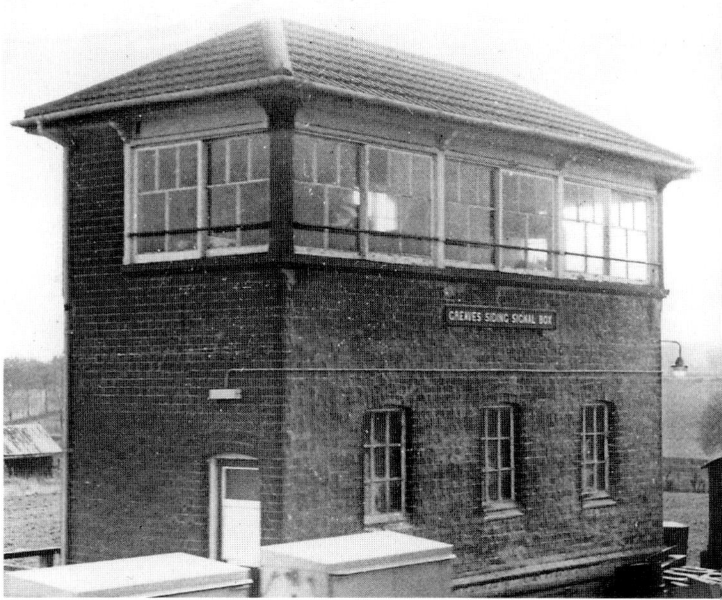

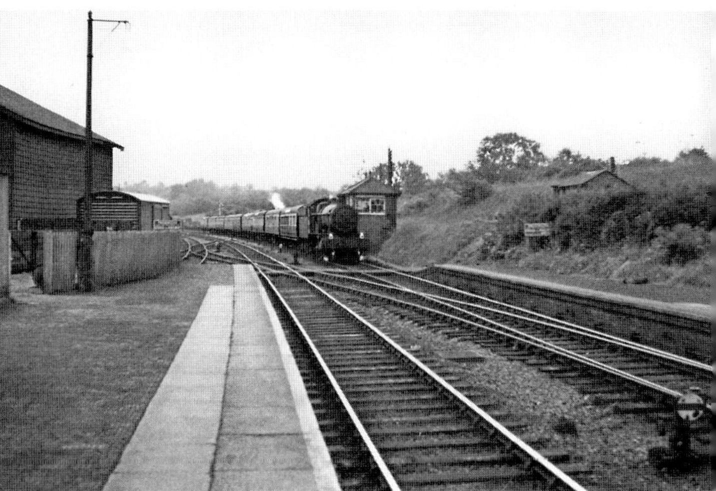

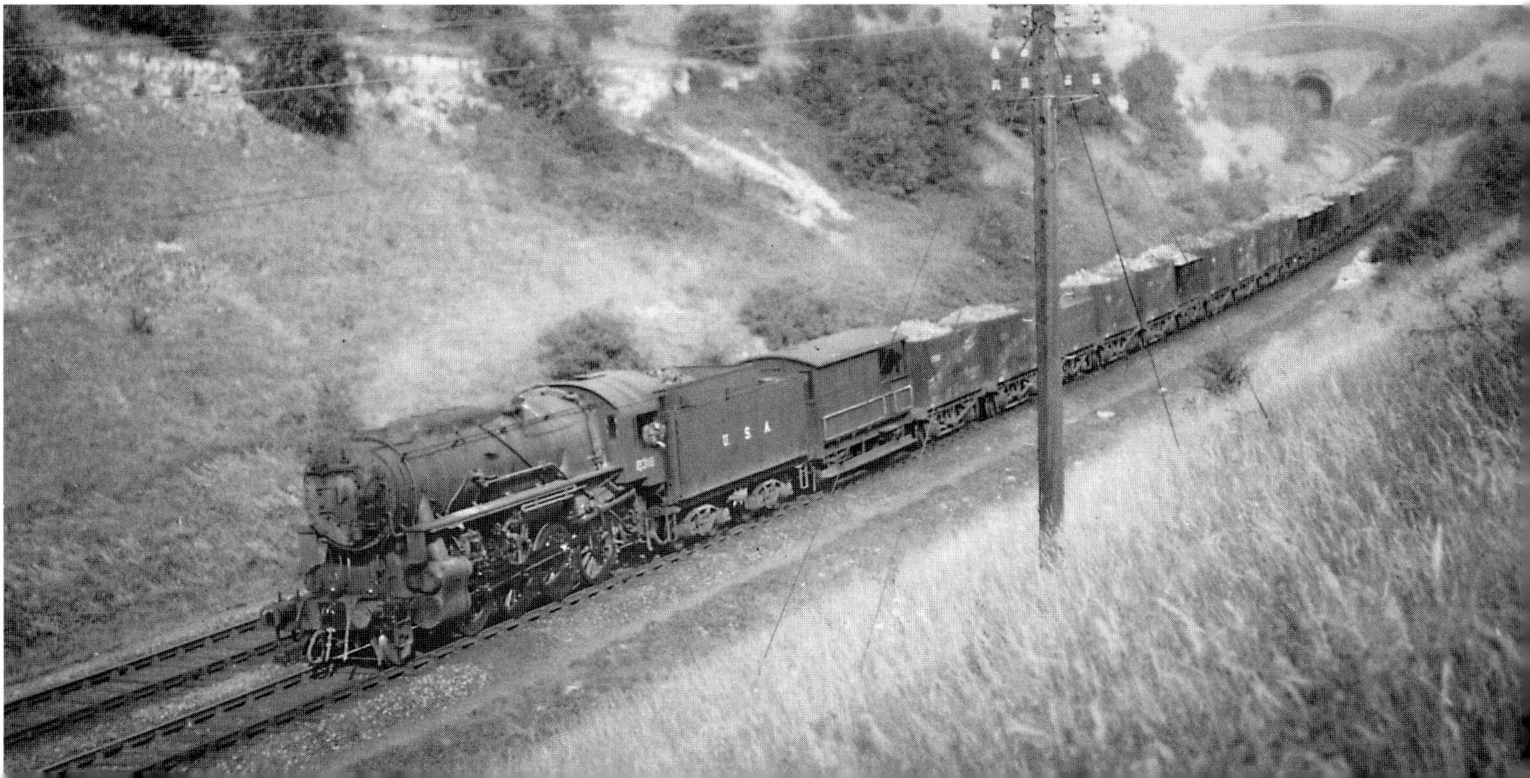

Above: **Leamington Shed, 18 September 1963**. Just before the line crossed the Warwick & Napton branch of the Grand Union Canal the GWR developed a loco shed, opened in September 1906 – it had the distinction of being the first of Churchward's standard type straight sheds. By the time of this view south, some of the carriage sidings, to the right of the shed, had been converted into a facility for refuelling diesel multiple units. Leamington was the outer limit for the Birmingham suburban service. To the right can just be made out a signal on the main line.

R S Carpenter collection

Below: **Leamington, circa 1902**. The original 1846 route of the Birmingham & Oxford Junction Railway actually bypassed the town, which, in 1851, had a population of 15,724, so was not to be ignored. Consequently, the GWR drew up revised plans and tried to reach an accommodation with the LNWR to share a station. But the latter, having opened earlier, was not interested. This resulted in the oldest station being on Avenue Road with the GWR station on Warwick Old Road, on the site of a large block of buildings on Eastnor Terrace. At opening the GWR station had a magnificent 270' train shed covering two carriage sidings and two platform faces. Shortly afterwards an 'excursion' platform was opened on the up side beyond the main train shed. This shed was removed sometime in the early 1890s. A 130 yards-long public footbridge was built across the northern ends of both stations soon after opening, although there was no access to the LNWR'S platforms, and the steps to the GWR's were later removed too.

Above: **Leamington, 1910**. At opening there were two lines on the north side that went round the train shed, used not only as up and down goods loops but the up line was intended for excursion traffic too. A connection was made to the adjacent LNWR's lines off the down loop and from 1908 a double junction between the GWR and LNWR facing Rugby allowed through running. Here, 'Chancellor' class 2-4-0 No.151 is transferring an LNWR horse box between the two sets of metals. The former excursion platform had by this time become a bay in its own right with a train shed over it. Both the up and down main platforms had also been extended with a bay being built into the north end of the down platform. *R S Carpenter collection*

Right, above: **Leamington Spa, 1914**. On 12 July 1913, the GWR added 'Spa' to the station name. The engine of this Bournemouth bound train which has LSWR coaches at the front is unrebuilt De Glehn compound, No.102 *La France*, one of the trio of these 4-4-2 engines. The wonderful bracket signal has two arms 'off' for the train – the top one controlled by South signal box which was perched on the north side of Bath Place viaduct – and the lower arm by the next box ahead – South Junction. The other pair of signals on this gantry controlled the up main line through the station. A tank engine can be glimpsed on the adjacent LNWR lines to the right. *R S Carpenter collection*

Right, below: **Leamington Spa, late 1930s**. The GWR decided to improve this important station in 1936. A contract worth £35,353 was awarded to Holliday & Greenwood for the new works. This involved widening and lengthening the platforms which also necessitated the removal of the remains of the canopies and the construction of new, better ones: the drainage was to their centres so that no rain would drip onto waiting passengers! This view of the down platform shows some coaches in the bay along with the old and new canopies. *GWR Magazine*

Above: **Leamington Spa, 1947**. The rebuilding in 1936/7 incorporated a three storey Portland stone faced set of period buildings on the down side opening to a 670' platform, with one of 650' on the main line side of an up island platform. Essentially the rebuilding involved the removal of the sloping approach to the buildings on the down side, taking away the earth and building a road level entrance directly from the Old Warwick Road. The company's name in full is proudly proclaimed at the top of the building with the station's name on the front of the canopy. On the right is the entrance to the subway that passes under the lines to the other side of the ex-LNWR lines. Leamington featured heavily in the GWR's selling of its services to, chiefly, American tourists in their quest for 'Shakespeareland'.

Mile Post 92½ Picture Library, A W V Mace collection

Below, left: **Leamington Spa General, 23 May 1953**. 4-6-0 No.4993 *Dalton Hall* eases an up freight through the station, the name of which had 'General' added in September 1950. From 1889 the up excursion platform was converted to goods loops. Prior to 1901, freight trains would have, when they had passed the 121 lever North signal box visible above the wagons, swung north and travelled behind the up platform, rejoining the main lines just south of the station before proceeding along Bath Place viaduct. Although the original train shed had four tracks under it, the middle two were meant to be carriage loops. With permission for the lengthening of the platforms in 1901 these two middle roads were altered to allow through running. Originally too the single road engine shed was on the down side beyond the signal box, but was replaced by a new depot south of the station in 1906. Carriage sidings were opened in 1910 on the site of the former engine shed. As the goods shed was on the down side just beyond the platforms, when these were enlarged, the freight side of operations had to be moved some two hundred and fifty yards north. This also allowed, from 1910, for a down bay, on the left.

E R Morten

Below, right: **Leamington Spa General, late 1950s**. Pulling into the down platform is an express hauled by No.6915 *Mursley Hall*. The coaches are passing across a series of viaducts over the rooftops of Leamington. The nearest is Bath Place, 80 yards long, then Clement Street, 91 yards, Court Street, 75 yards, and Neilson Street, 166 yards. Just south of these was the bridge over the canal. In the background the down bracket signals can be made out. Before the Great War, carriages for Stratford-upon-Avon were slipped from passing express trains. There was a signal for this by the canal bridge, the guard releasing the carriage at Court Street bridge, which then glided into the down platform after the express had passed through the station. Waiting for the signal to allow it to proceed on the up side is 4-cylinder 4-6-0 No.5029 *Shirburn Castle* on what looks like a fitted van freight.

Mile Post 92½ Picture Library, A W V Mace collection

Above: **Leamington, 31 August 1957**. Standing in the down bay platform on a parcels coach is 0-4-2T No.5813, with 'GWR' showing on the side tank and sporting an 82A, Bristol Bath Road, shed plate, though it had transferred from there to Leamington in April 1957. No.5813 was not around long, being withdrawn in November 1957 – it would be interesting to know it ever carried an 84D Leamington plate. This platform was used by trains to Stratford-upon-Avon and during January 1961 an unusual loco seen on some of the services was Hawksworth outside cylinder 0-6-0PT No.1507, running in after overhaul at Wolverhampton Works.

T E Williams

Oxford-Birmingham GWR working timetable June 1862

Broad and Narrow Gauge - down trains - weekdays - trains from Leamington and Warwick

TRAIN	FROM	TO	Dep	Notes: Narrow gauge trains in bold. Goods runs as required
ECS	Warwick	Stratford	7.50 am	
Passenger	Leamington	Wolverhampton	7.55am	
Passenger	Leamington	Wolverhampton	9.0am	
Passenger	Leamington	Wolverhampton	10.30am	
Passenger	Leamington	Stratford	12.25pm	
Passenger	Leamington	Wolverhampton	2.45 pm	
Goods	**Leamington**	**Wolverhampton**	**3.35 pm**	
Passenger	Leamington	Wolverhampton	7.45 pm	
Passenger	Leamington	Stratford	9.0 pm	

Broad and Narrow Gauge - up trains - weekdays - trains to Warwick and Leamington

TRAIN	FROM	TO	Dep	Notes: Narrow gauge trains in bold. Goods runs as required
Passenger	Stratford	Warwick	7.45 am	
Passenger	Wolverhampton	Leamington	9.55am	
Passenger	Wolverhampton	Leamington	11.55am	
Passenger	Stratford	Leamington	12.10 pm	
Passenger	Stratford	Leamington	1.40 pm	
Goods	**Wolverhampton**	**Warwick**	**2.35 pm**	
Passenger	Wolverhampton	Leamington	5.5 pm	
Passenger	Wolverhampton	Leamington	6.5pm	
Passenger	Stratford	Leamington	7.45 pm	
Passenger	Wolverhampton	Leamington	11.0 pm	

LNWR at Leamington Spa

Above: **Leamington Spa (Avenue), September 1947**. A branch from the London & Birmingham Railway main line at Coventry arrived at Milverton, to the west of Leamington, in December 1844. In 1846 the company, which became part of the LNWR, had authorisation to extend the branch from Milverton into Leamington and onto Rugby where it would meet the main line again, making the shortest route for passengers travelling from Leamington to London, albeit with a change of trains. The idea of a joint station for both LNWR and GWR did not materialise and so in March 1851 the former opened from Leamington to Rugby with a single line station next to The Avenue, over eighteen months before the GWR. A rail connection between the two companies was put in for the Warwick Agricultural show in 1859, consisting of a single line just north of the GWR station. When its station was enlarged, the GWR moved this connection to south of the station. Looking towards Rugby sees a motor train waiting for passengers with ex-LNWR 0-6-2T No.6683 in charge. *Millbrook House Ltd*

Left, above: **Leamington G W Junction box, 1958**. This view is along the LNWR line from Rugby towards Leamington. The ex-LNWR box existed due to the connection between the LNWR and GWR lines, off to the left beyond the canal bridge, which opened in July 1908. This permitted through running for coal trains, and empties, from the Rugby area to South Wales and the Midlands. *Patrick Kingston*

Left, below: **Southam & Long Itchington, 15 March 1958**. Pausing at the station on this single line to Daventry, which went off the Leamington-Rugby branch at Marton Junction, is Ivatt 2-6-2T No.41322. The passenger service never was intensive: in the years before closure only three trains a day went to Daventry and Weedon, on the London to Birmingham main line continuing to Blisworth, with just two reversing there before terminating at Northampton. With waits of over ten minutes at Blisworth the service was condemned to be poorly patronised. The line was comparatively late in opening, 1 August 1895, and closing to passengers on 15 September 1958. *H F Wheller collection*

Above: **Leamington Spa (Milverton), 1956**. Waiting at the 'standard' LNWR kit-type wooden station is an auto-train with Ivatt 2-6-2T No.41285. The station was opened by the LNWR in December 1844. Railway historian C R Clinker noted: 'The numerous changes made in the names of the LNW stations at Warwick and Leamington provide one of the most remarkable examples of station nomenclature in the country. ' It opened as Leamington, becoming Warwick (Milverton) around February 1854, Warwick around July 1856, reverting in 1857 to Warwick (Milverton), became Leamington (Milverton) about October 1860 and so on, finally renamed Leamington Spa (Milverton) for Warwick from February 1952 as shown here. The line to Coventry via Kenilworth is still an essential part of the cross-country network as it links the ex-GWR main line from the south to the ex-LNWR lines into Birmingham's New Street.

Brunel University, Mowat collection

Right, above: **Warwick, early 1950s**. The station was opened on the Birmingham & Oxford Junction Railway on 1 October 1852. Heading north is a fitted freight train hauled by Didcot based 2-6-0 No.6363. On the up platform is the signal box that opened in 1909, replacing one a few hundred yards north on the up side. At the same time the South signal box closed: it used to control the goods yard south of the station, but its duties were taken over by the new box. *R S Carpenter collection*

Right, below: **Warwick, 19 April 1963**. This clear view north shows two bracket signals: the down one is nicely silhouetted against the sky ensuring that it shows up well. On the down side accommodation was made for the Royal Agricultural Show in June 1892: the extra platform length can be seen as well as the 'temporary' platform on the left. The siding on the up side became a loop from 1944 controlled by the other bracket signal. The crossover allowed banking engines to regain the down siding on the left. *P J Garland collection*

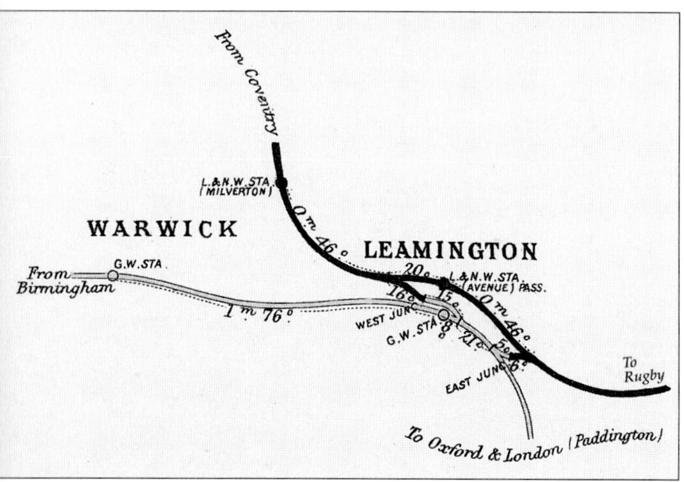

Above: **Warwick, 25 July 1943.** Waiting for its next banking duty in the bay is GWR '5101' class 2-6-2T No.5163. Many trains needed a helpful shove if they were to reach the top of Hatton Bank, two and three-quarter miles away up a gradient of 1 in 103. The banking loco was not attached to the train. After doing its duty, the banker was allowed 9 minutes to return to Warwick light engine. Freights were sometimes helped from Leamington to Hatton with the assisting loco attached in front of the train engine. The dip under the Canal Bridge between Leamington and Warwick had caused 'many instances where up and down freights have parted' according to the *Sectional Appendix to the Working Time Table*, so extra care was urged on drivers and guards in that area.   *V R Webster collection, Kidderminster Railway Museum*

Left, above: **Hatton bank, 6 October 1951.** With Leamington Spa being in a dip, a passage through it by up trains necessitates a descent followed by an ascent. Having come down from Harbury at about 1 in 187, the climb up from Hatton northwards is quite a lot stiffer, at 1 in 103/105 for much of the six miles with a short section at 1 in 100, Hatton station being at the top of the bank. Here a northbound train of loaded iron ore wagons, possibly from Wroxton quarry north of Banbury, is pulled north of Warwick by 85B Gloucester-based No.5948 *Siddington Hall* with a plume of smoke from the banker in the distance.   *Millbrook House Ltd*

Left, below: **RCH map of Leamington, 1914.** The GWR faced competition from the LNWR here for London traffic, but gradually the GWR improved its service to become faster than its rival even before the shorter route via Princes Risborough was constructed. As for Warwick, the LNWR claimed that its Milverton station, one and half miles away, was the one to use for that historic town.

Above: **Hatton, 5 September 1953**. Just about to pass through the station is 2-6-0 No.5330 with an express for Birmingham from the south coast – the reporting numbers appear to be in danger of falling off! A freight train lurks in the down goods loop. The railwayman is standing on the site of the South signal box closed in 1936.   *T E Williams*

Below: **Hatton station, 15 July 1962**. Another station which opened on 1 October 1852, it was adjacent to the Grand Union Canal in this rural part of Warwickshire. It became a junction for the single line to Stratford-upon-Avon from October 1860. Station buildings are off to the left and a lattice footbridge, once enclosed, links the platforms. Looking towards Warwick gives a good view of the rather spartan facilities here. In better times for the railway the station name board used to proclaim Hatton as 'Junction for Bearley, Alcester & Stratford-upon-Avon lines'. The platform mounted 75 lever signal box dates from 1936, replacing ones either end of the station. The train passing through on the down line is the 9.30am from Paddington with No.7026 *Tenby Castle* in charge.   *R K Blencowe collection*

Above: **Hatton South Junction, c.1948-1950**. This view taken from the road bridge at the north end of the station shows well the junction with the main line. Arriving from the south along the line from Stratford is an unidentified GWR railcar, of the second generation, with an auto trailer on a Leamington service. In the up loop, which was just a siding until 1901, is a freight train waiting its opportunity to join the up main line through the station. The two main lines can be seen curving away towards Lapworth above the auto coach. *Joe Moss collection*

Line to Stratford-upon-Avon

Below: **Claverdon, 1959**. This delightful station with symmetrical waiting shelters is on the route from Hatton to Stratford-upon-Avon. When opened in 1860 the single line had just one platform and a siding which, in 1884, was converted into a loop. Another platform was provided but, in practice, was used for unloading coal and other goods. When the line was doubled just prior to the start of World War 2 this new station, eight chains closer to Hatton was opened: history has repeated itself with the line singled since 1968, with only the up platform used, but retaining the shelter. Shakespeare's town now enjoys probably more direct trains to London than it ever has, 5 up and 4 down running into Marylebone station. Since privatisation of the railways in the 1990s passenger journeys nationwide have seen a substantial rise. Currently, one train per day makes the journey along the Lapworth to Claverdon side of the Hatton triangle thus keeping it open for technical purposes. *Stations UK*

Right: **Hatton West Junction, 15 April 1950**. Bringing a freight train round the curve from Hatton station is Collett 2-8-0 No.3815 heading towards Claverdon and Stratford. Controlling events is West Junction signal box, called Branch Junction until 1939. The junction dates from July 1897 with the opening of the North Curve, which passes away to the left under the magnificent bracket signal post, enabling trains to go direct from Stratford towards Birmingham. While the tallest post is for Hatton, the next is for Lapworth, with the small, single arm controlling access to a down loop around the North Curve. *Millbrook House Ltd*

Below: **Hatton North Junction, circa 1936.** A view from the footbridge depicts a Birmingham-bound express which has just whizzed through the station and is approaching the North Junction. On the right are the lines that make the North Curve towards Stratford-upon-Avon. To the left is the commencement of the up loop, with catch points for runaway wagons.
A T Cooke collection, Kidderminster Railway Museum

Slip coaches detached from Oxford-Birmingham trains – October 1879			
Train	**Slipped at**	**Time**	**Note**
3.30pm London-Wolverhampton	Banbury	6.6pm	
6.30pm London-Wolverhampton	Banbury	8.45pm	
6.30pm London-Wolverhampton	Knowle	9.33pm	
7.5am Wolverhampton-London	Warwick	7.56am	For Stratford branch
6.20am Birkenhead-London	Hatton	10.30am	
6.20am Manchester-London	Knowle		3rd Wednesday of month
10.2am Manchester-London	Hatton		For Stratford branch
10.2am Manchester-London	Fenny Compton	4.32pm	Saturdays
12.10pm Manchester-Leamington	Hatton	5.37pm	

Left: **Rowington troughs.** GWR outside framed 0-6-0 No.354 heads a northbound freight train over the 560 yards-long water troughs. This engine, last of its class in service, was no stranger to the area being allocated to Tyseley in 1921 and Leamington by 1934, being withdrawn later that year. The force of water missing the scoop of engines using the troughs and overflowing onto the ballast could be quite a nuisance as constant maintenance was needed to restore the track bed. Some railway companies overcame this problem by putting old sleepers at right angles to the ones supporting the tracks so protecting the ballast. Note the distinctive water tank through the arch for topping up the troughs.   *Real Photographs*

Below: **Rowington Junction.** Just over two and a half miles north of Hatton was the junction for the three and a half mile branch to Henley-in-Arden. Although authorised in 1861, it was not until 1894 that motor trains started to shuttle between the terminus there and Lapworth. However, with the building of the North Warwickshire line from Tyseley to Stratford-upon-Avon in 1906, a new through station was built. The old station area became goods only and a spur between the old and new stations meant that from 1908 until 1915, the town was served by passenger trains from both Moor Street and Lapworth. The line curving off to the right past the signal box was closed, although it was used for wagon storage, and lifted beyond the road bridge soon after the service from Lapworth was stopped. The signal box lasted, probably as a summer block post, until 1957.   *Philip Hopkins*

Lapworth to Birmingham

Left: **Lapworth.** A station called Kingswood was opened here by the GWR in 1854. From 1894 the platforms were lengthened to give a staggered arrangement with bay platforms. In 1902 the station name was changed to Lapworth. This view, looking south in about 1910, shows the arrival of an auto-train from Henley-in-Arden. After depositing passengers it will reverse to wait in the bay over on the left under the fine covered footbridge. The bay on the right is for Birmingham trains.   *Author's collection*

Above: **Lapworth**. This view looking north in 1929 shows the 1894 signal box under the footbridge with the Henley bay on the right.

Clarence Gilbert, R S Carpenter collection

Below: **Lapworth, 1960**. A plan to provide four running lines from Rowington Junction to Olton, where, since 1907, the route had been quadruple to Tyseley, was drafted before the Great War but hostilities and then the general economic situation meant that it was not revived until the unemployment relief schemes of the late 1920s. £400,000 was the cost for eight miles of new trackwork to Olton, with the layout seen below, looking north, being built in 1933. The section between here and Rowington Junction was never done. The two main lines are to the right, with crossovers allowing transfers to the relief lines between the 1932 signal box and the bridge in the distance. The two facing signals have route indicators in the white boxes under the arms.

R S Carpenter collection

Left, above: **Knowle, 1891**. Opened by the Birmingham & Oxford Junction Railway on 1 October 1852, this picture looking towards Birmingham was taken the year before both platforms were extended northwards. In between the lines is a water column. The space left by the removal of broad gauge lines is quite noticeable. The station buildings and chimneys on the left and the shelter for the up platform, on the right, are highly decorative. *Author's collection*

Left, below: **Knowle & Dorridge, 1959**. The latter place was added to the station's name from 1 July 1899. Looking towards Birmingham shows the platform curvature and the extensive awnings: just visible is the covered footbridge. From 1933 the station operated with four platform faces, fast to the right (the original pair) and relief to the left. *Stations UK*

Below: **Knowle & Dorridge, 1951**. About to shatter the early evening quiet is an express bound for Paddington hauled by No.5014 *Goodrich Castle*. On the right, beyond the GWR water tower, was an extensive goods yard later used as sidings for car carrier trains, encouraging people to put their vehicles onto a train to Cornwall and elsewhere. Also of note is the provision of up and down goods loops even with the quadruple track. The station was renamed Knowle from 6 May 1968 and changed again, becoming Dorridge from 6 May 1974. *Millbrook House Ltd*

Above: **Bentley Heath Crossing, before 1914**. Just over half a mile north of Knowle & Dorridge station was a level crossing, Mill Lane, where a southbound express approaches hauled by 'Saint' class 4-6-0 No.2909 *Lady of Provence*. As stated, the line was quadrupled in 1933. In the background is an occupation bridge from the farm that gave the crossing its name. A small, 15 lever, box was opened in 1875 to control events here.   *Author's collection*

Below: **Bentley Heath Crossing, 11 September 1948**. Photographed from the crossing looking north is a south-bound train including Southern carriages hauled by No.7008 *Swansea Castle*. Note the loco's front number is still on the bufferbeam, GWR style, though it has 'British Railways' on its tender. The small arm on the bracket signal is for trains going into the up goods loop. The up relief signals are prominent above the road bridge. The larger, 49 lever, signal box provided here in 1932 closed on 1 September 1969 when a new power box opened at Saltley.

Millbrook House Ltd

Above: **Bentley Heath Crossing, 24 May 1959.** 2-8-0 No.3803 of 85B Gloucester is heading north on the down main with an empty wagon train. This was a popular spot for photographers, having a fine stretch of well signalled quadruple track where expresses could be seen at speed and long freight trains occupied the fast lines. Beyond the footbridge were the goods loops for both directions, so heavy was the traffic. Just under the footbridge was a connection from the down relief to a Ministry of Supply cold store depot opened during World War 2. *M Mensing*

Left, above: **Widney Manor, early 1960s.** This is the view towards Birmingham along the up main platform. It illustrates well the way that the GWR looked after its passengers. The footbridge, originally covered, was accessed by steps that started under the awnings on the platforms. Thus passengers could buy a ticket, emerge onto the platform and walk across the footbridge to another platform, all under cover. When the lines were quadrupled, the down platform became an island, and a new down relief platform was built to the left of it. The signal box, between the running lines, had 27 levers. *Lens of Sutton collection*

Left, below: **Widney Manor, 1920.** The bracket signal has just been reset after the passage of a Birmingham-Leamington stopping train hauled by inside cylinder 2-6-2T No.3913. This was one of a class of 20 locos, converted from 'Dean Goods' 0-6-0 tender engines, built specially for Birmingham suburban services following opening of the North Warwickshire line. It was to the left of the train that the extra pair of lines were laid in 1933. North of the station on the up side can be seen the unassuming goods yard accessed by a trailing single slip from the down line and trailing point to the up main line. Facilities consisted of a sizeable brick shed, complete with loading gauge, as well as a cattle and loading bay. Twice a day saw train activity in the goods yard with, in the morning, the 8.25am Bordesley to Oxford calling and, soon after noon, the 10.15am Leamington to Tyseley. *R S Carpenter collection*

Above: **Solihull.** A wonderful picture at the original station with an up stopping train headed by 'Flower' class 4-4-0 No.4149 *Auricula*. Opened on 1 October 1852 the platforms were lengthened at the Birmingham end in 1890.

R K Blencowe collection

Right, above: **Solihull, 17 June 1929.** Looking south towards Knowle shows the footbridge still has its fine cover. Prior to World War 2, down trains carried a slip coach for this important station. The ivy covered signal box, in this position since 1890, had 29 levers. Its 1933 replacement, west of the relief lines on the edge of the embankment, was a much bigger affair with 74 levers. *Clarence Gilbert, R S Carpenter collection*

Right, below: **Solihull, mid 1950s.** A different solution to the opportunities presented by quadrupling was developed at Solihull. Two island platforms were built, one, numbered 1 and 2, with the main lines around it and the other, 3 and 4, with the relief lines either side. No.5950 *Wardley Hall* hauls a perishables train from Plymouth on the down main line. The up and down relief lines were removed in July 1968. *R S Carpenter collection*

Solihull, 25 July 1961. Three of the four tracks are occupied in this view. Large Prairie tank No.4167 is in charge of an up mixed local freight while on the adjacent line is the 4.10pm Paddington - Birkenhead express and further to the left is the empty stock of the 5.38pm Birmingham Snow Hill-Knowle & Dorridge, showing the problem of some rush-hour commuter trains - being needed in one direction only. Of course by this date most local services around here were diesel multiple units, with locos and carriages brought out for peak time trains.

M Mensing

Above: **Olton, circa 1927**. Storming through the up platform on its way to Oxford is an express hauled by an unidentified 'Atbara' class 4-4-0. Just north of the station the line crosses Richmond Road, beyond it is the signal box visible behind the rear coaches and the start of quadruple lines north to Tyseley. The bracket signal for down trains can be made out on the left, just under the canopy. At enlargement in 1907, the new relief lines were laid outside the up and down main. However, from 1913 the junction here was altered so that the relief lines were operated as a pair south of the main lines. Olton's signal box closed in 1933. *Clarence Gilbert, R S Carpenter collection*

Right, above: **Olton, March 1948**. The four lines from Birmingham stopped short of Olton station until 1933 when the GWR made four lines south to Lapworth. The former up platform became sandwiched by the fast lines with the relief lines around the old down platform. This external view along Station Drive shows the new platforms behind the station entrance building, which is complete with the company name. *R S Carpenter collection*

Right, below: **Olton, August 1962**. Still on express passenger work after thirty-six years of use is one of the original 'Castle' class 4-6-0s, No.4096 *Highclere Castle* – though it did not have long to go before withdrawal in January 1963. It is heading north with a train of Southern Region coaches, possibly from Bournemouth. Olton was only ever only a passenger station, with no goods yard. The photographer is standing on the up relief platform. *Joe Moss collection*

Above: **Acocks Green & South Yardley, 1905**. When first opened on 1 October 1852, this station was a typical two platform affair and there were no freight facilities. The *Illustrated London News*, reporting on the opening of the line, mentioned the area as being called Haycocks Green! Looking towards Olton shows an excursion train about to enter the well patronised down platform: note the wide gap between the two lines – again a legacy from broad gauge days. The station was included in the 1907 quadrupling and the GWR enlarged the station in the same way as at Olton and Solihull, laying new lines outside the original pair and making the existing platforms into islands. From 1907 to 1913 lines were paired, from the north side, as: up relief; up main; down main; down relief. *R S Carpenter collection*

Left, above: **Acocks Green & South Yardley, circa 1910-1912**. With the enlargement the GWR built this access from Sherbourne Road in the days when most people walked to the station. Workmen are just putting the finishing touches to the forecourt.

R S Carpenter collection

Left, below: **Acocks Green & South Yardley, mid 1960s**. In 1913 the GWR altered the running arrangement of the lines here – the northern pair changed from up relief and up main to up relief and down main. Nicely framed by the roofless footbridge is a down express, 1O24, from the Southern Region, headed by an ex-LMS Class Five 4-6-0 which probably took over at Oxford. The up main line is to the right, alongside the other island platform. The station became simply 'Acocks Green' from 6 May 1968 with the relief lines being taken out of use in that year.

Mile Post 92¹/₂ Picture Library, A W V Mace collection

The North Warwickshire Line

Above: **Hall Green station, late 1920s**. Although being connected to the Oxford, Worcester & Wolverhampton Railway via Honeybourne since 1859, and to the Birmingham & Oxford Railway via Hatton since 1861, Stratford-upon-Avon was still a railway backwater. As the GWR had opened a section of line from Cheltenham to Honeybourne in 1906 two objectives could be achieved by building a direct Birmingham to Stratford line. Not only could it capture the commuter market from the town but also become part of a wider picture, giving the GWR its own independent route from Birmingham towards Bristol and the West Country. Thus the line through north Warwickshire and improvements to the OWW link became strategically important to the GWR, as well as providing additional revenue. First along the line, opened in July 1908, was Spring Road Platform while the first substantial station was here at Hall Green. In this posed picture probably all the employees have been summoned. It illustrates not only the all male staff at that time – a situation changed by the Great War – but also the range and numbers employed at a simple station. Work may have been long and the pay modest but it was steady and reliable employment in a difficult world.

Lens of Sutton

Below: **Henley-in-Arden, 1906**. This demonstrates how lines were built just after the turn of the century, with the North Warwickshire line under construction just north of the site of the new Henley-in-Arden station at Crockets Farm bridge. The constructors have laid a single track along which horses pulled wagons. A steam navvy does most of the work but a substantial number of workers are still needed for the fine tuning of the work on the cutting.

G M Perkins, R S Carpenter collection

Left, above: **Tyseley, 28 July 1928.** Looking south shows the junction of the North Warwickshire line, curving away to the right, with the Birmingham & Oxford line heading to the left. Although built for quadruple track operation, for the first three months after opening in October 1906, there were only two tracks through the station; it was not until January 1907 that there were four tracks from just north of the station to north of Olton station, a distance of about two miles. In the middle of the picture is the large, 127 lever, South signal box flanked by the down relief on the right and up relief on the left. The down and up main lines are further to the left, either side of the tall signal post. On the extreme right is a bracket signal with shunting hoops on the three arms.
Clarence Gilbert, R S Carpenter collection

Left, below: **Tyseley station, circa 1908.** Note the covered steps leading from the street level booking office to just under the canopy on the platform thus giving the passenger continuous protection from the elements. At the down relief platform a steam rail motor rests, probably before continuing its journey to Birmingham from the North Warwickshire line. The next line over was, at this date, the down main, but became the up relief in 1913 when the direction of the lines was changed.
Lens of Sutton

Below: **Tyseley station, exterior, 25 April 1970.** The station was opened by the GWR on 1 October 1906 where the road bridge crossed the lines. The buildings are very similar to those at, for example, Olton and Acocks Green. More recently the station has been restored to its 'original' condition due to its proximity to the Tyseley Locomotive Works Visitor Centre on the site of the old steam loco shed.
M A King

Above: **Tyseley, 30 October 1954**. After June 1913 the up and down main lines passed either side of the north platform while the two relief lines did likewise at the south platform. Passing through the station on the down main with the 'Cambrian Coast Express' the driver of 'Britannia' class 4-6-2 No.70018 *Flying Dutchman* will be keeping a keen watch on his speed on the approach to Snow Hill station, some three miles ahead. This famous named train called at selected stations in Wales including Welshpool, Moat Lane Junction and Machynlleth before terminating at Aberystwyth, a journey of over 250 miles from Paddington. *G W Sharpe*

Below: **Tyseley yard**. Not only was there an impressive junction at Tyseley but also a set of goods sidings from where the engine is emerging. Around to the south of the sidings were a pair up and down goods loops, which are seen passing to the left. Both sets of lines are controlled by the fine bracket signals complete with shunting hoops. The station is off to the right where a passenger train has passed by. Apparently the grounded coach body was known by staff as 'Pneumonia Cabin'! And also here at Tyseley are extensive engine sheds.

Brian Moone collection, Kidderminster Railway Museum

The allocation at 84E Tyseley in February 1954

0-6-0	4	4-6-0	17
2-8-0	7	2-6-0	14
2-6-2T	20	0-6-2T	4
0-6-0PT	29	0-6-0 Diesel	29
		Total	**124**

Above: **Tyseley shed coal stage, 16 June 1951**. As well as two roundhouses there was also a very large elevated coal stage that could be utilised from either side. On top was a massive water tank to supply the numerous water columns in the area. Interestingly, the stage has a massive canvas 'curtain' – possibly a throwback to the blackout days of wartime or perhaps merely protection from the weather. 'Bulldog class 4-4-0 No.3454 *Skylark* has worked up from its Didcot home.   *R S Carpenter collection*

Left, above: **Tyseley shed, 1964.** Accommodation and servicing of GWR engines in the Birmingham area has been carried out at several places. As traffic grew so did the demand for more room and a move from Birmingham to Bordesley occurred in 1855. This sufficed until 1908 when continual expansion, not least the opening of the North Warwickshire line, meant another move, to Tyseley. After official closure to steam in November 1966 it became a diesel stabling point; a new diesel depot had already been opened here in July 1958. But steam continued to visit well into 1967, particularly to use the wheel turning facilities. More lately, the engine shed has been the home of Tyseley Locomotive Works. This view from the ramp up to the double sided coaling stage shows the shed in the background with the carriage sidings to the left.   *Author's collection*

Left, below: **Tyseley shed roundhouse, 22 November 1964.** There were two turntables inside the buildings each with 28 radiating tracks. A range of engines is on show here, including 0-6-0PT Nos.3770 and 4635, 0-6-2T No.5684, 2-6-2T 'Prairie' tank No.4179 and mixed traffic 4-6-0 No.6859 *Yiewsley Grange.* Having all been serviced and turned they are stabled with their chimneys under the smoke cowls, ready for duty. In the early 1930s and in later years, Tyseley was home to seven 28XX 2-8-0 engines for heavy freights between Birmingham and the capital.   *Millbrook House Ltd*

Above: **Tyseley goods shed**. Just getting into its stride is an up express being hauled by the one of the early 'Castles' No.4079 *Pendennis Castle*, as viewed from the end of the relief platform at Tyseley. Although painted out as a war time expedient, the lettering on the goods shed still shows through – it used to proclaim 'GWR goods shed. Express goods train services one day transit between important towns'. The train is on the up main. The two bracket signals for down trains have the most important route on the tallest post, which is straight ahead to Snow Hill, while the lesser route, using the crossovers, is for Moor Street.

B P Hoper collection

Right, above: **Small Heath and Sparkbrook, early 1900s**. A typical two platform affair was opened by the GWR in 1863 and lengthened at the Tyseley end in 1890. This view north shows that although there was a booking office on the Golden Hillock Road overbridge, there were also fine brick-built waiting rooms on both platforms.

R S Carpenter collection

Right, below: **Small Heath and Sparkbrook, 1929**. Although four lines were built from Tyseley south to Olton in 1907, and extended north in readiness for the opening of the loco shed the next year, quadrupling through this station was around late 1912 / early 1913. This operation made both platforms into islands. Due to the volume of traffic between the various goods yards in the area, the GWR opened a pair of goods lines, seen on the left with a down transfer freight, as well as an up good loop on the extreme right.

Clarence Gilbert, R S Carpenter collection

Above: **Bordesley Yard, 1954.** Small Heath Bridge is visible passing across all the tracks in the background. The six main running lines divide the area into two. On the right is the 'Caledonia Yard', part of which was developed from the site of an engine shed prior to Tyseley's opening in 1908. On the left of the running lines is the 'Old Yard', 'Baltic' and 'Baulks' yards. Early BR diesel shunters ply their trade on both sides, complete with shunter's trucks. As the GWR and the Midland Railway lines cross behind the picture at right angles, it was recognised right from early days that a connection would be in both their interests. So a single line spur to the Midland Railway's Camp Hill line was opened in November 1861; doubling did not take place until eighty years later during World War 2. Three reception loops were also built for transfer freights, Saltley engines often doing the work. This is now one of the chief routes for trains from New Street to Leamington.

Author's collection

Left, above: **View from Bordesley station, 20 July 1961.** Here the GWR main line passed under the MR tracks from the Camp Hill line to Saltley. Many trains in the opposite direction needed a banker due to the gradient here, 1 in 85 for over a mile. Looking from the end of the platforms shows Class Five 4-6-0 No.44816 drifting down the gradient towards Saltley on a fitted freight. Bordesley Junction, where the connecting spur from Bordesley Yard comes in, is immediately in front of the train with St. Andrews less than half a mile more then Landor Street a stone's throw further on.

M Mensing

Left, below: **Bordesley, 26 July 1929.** Looking south towards Leamington shows the MR line going across the GWR. At the end of the relief platform the signal gantry shows three possible routes – the left hand signals for the fast line, the middle ones for the relief road and the single arm for the goods yards at Small Heath. So busy was the area that a separate goods line was put in, presumably for trains destined for transfers between Small Heath sidings and Moor Street goods yard.

Clarence Gilbert, R S Carpenter collection

Right: **Bordesley station and entrance**. A passenger station opened in 1855, at the commencement of the curve towards Curzon Street, north of the Coventry Road bridge. It closed on 7 March 1915, being replaced by a new station on that date, a couple of hundred yards south. The development of Moor Street in July 1909, just before the tunnel to the main GWR station in the city, Snow Hill, resulted in the lines from north of Bordesley station being quadrupled from 1913 and through the station from 1915. A GWR commuter train from Moor Street has just passed over the 797 yard, 58 arch viaduct to arrive at the down relief island platform. The slightly staggered main line island platforms, 1 & 2, are on the right.
Rail Archive Stephenson; M A King

Below: **Duddeston Viaduct, 18 August 1949**. When railways were first developed in this area, the original plan was for the Birmingham & Oxford Junction Railway to curve north and join the Grand Junction Railway at Curzon Street. To do that it would have to cross, on the flat, the lines of the London & Birmingham Railway. With the Birmingham & Derby Junction Railway and the Birmingham & Gloucester Railway also vying to establish themselves in the Curzon Street area, needless to say it was a very congested place. The politics of the day meant that even though the viaduct to take this line to Curzon Street was built in early 1853, the connection with the LNWR station was never laid; lines on it were just used for sidings. New powers in the Birmingham & Oxford Junction (Birmingham Extension) Act stopped any connections with the LNWR and made the line proceed to a station at Great Charles Street in the city centre. Today, over 150 years later, the 355 yard Duddeston Viaduct still towers over the streets and workshops with the words 'Bordesley Cattle Station GWR'. *Millbrook House Ltd*

Birmingham's GWR stations

Above: **Moor Street, exterior, 12 April 1969.** Looking up the slope of Moor Street which allows the road to clear the railway lines underneath shows the modest entrance to the station that opened on 1 July 1909. The metal grill was necessary as the station was closed on Sundays. At the beginning of the last century the GWR station at Snow Hill was beset by problems. There was a bottleneck from the south with a stiff gradient, and unlike its LNWR and MR neighbours, there was no real alternative route for goods trains. With the development of the North Warwickshire line in 1908 Snow Hill was going to be overwhelmed and so Moor Street was constructed – it could be looked upon as an extension half a mile away! *M A King*

Below: **Moor Street, concourse, circa 1930.** Once inside the building there was a reasonable sized concourse that fed two, later three, platforms. Built on the down side of the main lines, Moor Street originally could be considered as the terminus of the two relief lines. Although chiefly used as a suburban station, due to its proximity to the city centre, it was also the departure point for some excursion trains. Platform length was a restriction though. With the reinstatement of passenger services into the 'new' Snow Hill station from 1987 up and down through platforms were built at Moor Street for these trains, though the bay platforms were taken out of use. However, the station has recently been renovated by a train operator that wants to reinstate the rail connections to the bays for running off-peak trains. *Brunel University Transport Collection, Clinker Views*

INSTRUCTIONS FOR WORKING TRAVERSING TABLES ON Nos. I, 2, 3 and 4 LINES.

1. The Traversers are worked by an Electric Controller fixed near the Stop Blocks, and the Operating or Commercial Department is responsible for manipulating them. The Handle is locked electrically from the Signal Box, and cannot be worked when the Signals are lowered for a train to run to the Platform Line affected.

2. Trains except Multiple Diesel units must be stopped short of the Traverser. The Porter or Shunter must uncouple the Engine, and it must then be run on to the Table on receipt of a hand signal from the Porter or Shunter.

3. The Operating or Commercial Department man working the Traverser must give the prescribed rings on the Telephone to the Signalman, who must then release the Lock, and after tht code has been acknowledged, and the Indicator shows that the Lock is off, the man manipulating the Traverser must operate Hand Plunger to form an electric contact, and then push the vertical lever from him to its fullest extent. The Controller handle must then be carefully moved by the man in charge for the purpose of traversing the Engine from one Line to the other.

4. After the Engine has becn removed from the Table, the Traverser must be returned to its normal position, the vertical lever being drawn back. The man manipulating the Traverser must then give the prescribed rings on the Telephone, indicating that the Traverser is not further required, and the Signalman must acknowledge the code by repeating it, and re-lock the Table.

5. A Disc works with each Traverser to show when the Table has returned to its normal position. This Disc shows a Red and Green Signal.

6. When a Train or Engine arrives which has to be traversed and the Table is then not in the correct position for the operation, the man in charge about to work the Traverser must inform the Engineman what he is going to do.

Moor Street, 1957. In steam days there were no platforms on the main line, which continued north over the southern approaches to New Street, into the tunnel and onto Snow Hill. Looking from the concourse shows 2-6-2T No.5181 at the head of a typical suburban train. On the right is the other face of the long platforms with the shorter platform 1 to the left. The wagon hoist that allowed access to the goods depot looms large over the railings of platform 1. To the left of that is a bracket signal that enabled up trains to pass along the main line or the relief lines, the latter indicated by the right hand pair of arms. The controlling signal box can be glimpsed beyond the end of No.5181's train.

Stations UK

Above: **The GWR's Birmingham Station and Great Western Hotel**. The railway from Oxford came in high over the rooftops of Bordesley, passed into a short cutting and proceeded northwards over the likes of Great Charles, Lionel, Water and Henrietta Streets. A mixed gauge station on Monmouth Street, later Colmore Row, was opened by the Birmingham & Oxford Junction Railway on 1 October 1852, the sloping site being sandwiched between Snow Hill and Livery Street. Work had begun on the site only since the start of that year. Later the approach cutting from the south was converted into brick arches to form a tunnel, of about 596 yards, into the station. The line north to Wolverhampton was not opened for another two years. This picture shows the station soon after completion of the 1912 rebuilding with the new arched entrance utilising part of the old 'Great Western Hotel' which was built over the approach lines in 1863. The closed hotel was taken over to house the railway offices connected with running such a large enterprise. The old building was demolished in 1969. While the company may have called its station 'Snow Hill' from around 1868, it took until after World War 2 for the platform nameboards to show this: it was just the GWR station to most people. *Author's collection*

Right, above: A 1939 plan to open a new station hotel on the site of the old one became shelved due to the war and never came to fruition. *Author's collection*

Right, below: **Livery Street, Birmingham, 1950**. When the station was rebuilt in 1871, due to the opportunity provided by removal of the broad gauge, it was decided to build two platforms with four tracks between them. The entrance on Snow Hill was to the up platform and this one in Livery Street was to the down platform, connected by a footbridge in the middle. A pair of scissors crossovers meant that both 450' platforms could hold two trains. *Birmingham Reference Library*

Above: **Snow Hill reconstruction, 1910**. Struggling to cope with the 350 to 400 trains per day here, the company decided to rebuild the station again, from 1906. A vast constraint upon this project was the tunnel approach from the south. Consequently it was decided to build Moor Street station some half a mile south to accommodate, chiefly, suburban trains. Snow Hill itself became two very long island platforms with long bays at the northern end. While all this was going on, 'Badminton' class 4-4-0 No.3294 *Blenheim* waits at the down platform. To some people the station was the 'GWR version of Crystal Palace'.   *R S Carpenter collection*

Below: **Snow Hill, 1962**. The two new island platforms were nearly three times the length of the previous ones at 1,188' – down main, and 1,197' – up main. Two through lines were made between them to allow for stock transfers as well as numerous freight trains which had no alternative route. Standing on the down main platform 5, leading to platform 6, shows a busy up main platform 7, with platform 8 in the distance, complete with two tone brick buildings and magnificent clock. A subway connected the up and down sides as well as stairs from the enlarged Colmore Row entrance.   *R K Blencowe collection*

Above: **Snow Hill, circa 1953.** Illustrating well the length of the island platforms is this northbound express at platform 5 headed by 4-6-0 No.1000 *County of Middlesex* of 84K Chester shed and the only double chimney member of the class at the time. The train has come to a stop so that the 1st class coaches at the rear are nearest to the steps to the station exit. The front of the train, technically in platform 6, has just gone beyond the crossovers from the platform line to the down through line to the left. Such movements were controlled by the small signals under the station roof by the first coach The crossovers were removed in the early 1960s. To accommodate suburban trains that terminated here, each island platform had two bays at the northern ends. Over on the left a tank engine and coaches has arrived at platform 9.

R S Carpenter collection

Below: **Snow Hill, 15 September 1956.** Waiting to depart south is Wolverhampton Stafford Road based 2-6-2T No.3104. Apart from creating long platforms, the 1906-10 enlargement also made up and down relief platforms around the main ones. This one is platform 12, formerly 11 until 1929; on the other side of the glazing was Snow Hill. Note the cowl above the engine so that the smoke could be vented without it fouling the air in the train shed. Over the platforms there were two types of roof. For the first 500' or so from the main entrance was a tall ridge and furrow glazed roof, at ninety degrees to the platforms and buildings below them, as shown here. This had a gap over the two through lines for air circulation. Over the rest of the platforms, including the bays, were ordinary glazed canopies. The station was completely reglazed in 1946 – air raids in 1940/1 had shattered much of the original.

H C Casserley

Above: **Snow Hill, 1958**. Amidst the hustle and bustle of expresses for London, the West Country, Birkenhead and Wales, the station was also host to some humbler trains, like the 'Dudley Dodger'. Now one of the largest parts of the West Midlands devoid of any rail passenger connections Dudley was once served by push-pull services with 0-4-2Ts, such as No.1438 here. Note the nameboard just states 'Birmingham'. The signals for up trains to pass along the through line, bypassing platform 8, and then accessing platform 7 can be seen sticking out from the canopy.

Author's collection

Below: **Snow Hill, 27 April 1963**. Looking down the steps shows a hive of activity on a special day for soccer fans and railway enthusiasts – Manchester United played Southampton in an F A Cup Semi-final at Villa Park and there were no less than 13 specials from the south coast, of which all but one had Southern Pacific motive power. Oblivious to the occasion is a freight with 2-6-2T No.4172 on the up through line. Just about to disgorge fans onto platform 7 at about 12.20pm is a special double-headed by ex-LMS Stanier 2-8-0 No.48417 and ex-SR rebuilt Pacific 34039 *Boscastle*. Meanwhile over on the down side rests ex-SR unrebuilt 'West Country' class 4-6-2 No. 34094 *Mortehoe*. Nine of the specials came up the main line from Oxford, with three via Oxford, Worcester and Stourbridge, (all needing pilot loco assistance from the latter) and the other, with 34094, over the Somerset & Dorset line, Gloucester and Stratford-upon-Avon.

Mile Post 92¹/₂ Picture Library, A W V Mace collection

Above: **Snow Hill, 29 August 1931**. Another part of the alterations in 1906-10 involved making some sidings to the north-east of the main line. While the main carriage sidings were south between Bordesley and Tyseley, there was a need for some storage facility and engine servicing north of the station near to the bay platforms. Accessed by means of a long ladder crossover from the down bays, platforms 3 & 4, across the four running lines and linking with the up bays, platforms 9 & 10, was a turntable and sidings at Northwood Street, near to where the four main lines disappeared into the Hockley tunnels. The servicing facilities are behind the train which is about to enter the up main platforms, 8 & 7, as indicated by the bracket signal. Heading the train is 'Bulldog' class 4-4-0 No.3406 *Calcutta*. Note the standard water tank in the background which supplied the water columns in the station as well as those by the turntable. *L Hanson*

Below: **Snow Hill**. While the north end of the down platform of the original station would have been almost on top of Great Charles Street, the same platform in the twentieth century station had been extended over Great Charles and Lionel Streets and almost over Water Street. The wonderful raised Birmingham North Signal Box is seen beyond the platform. In the distance are the Hockley tunnels accommodating the main and relief lines in two bores. Emerging from them, and being given the road along the up through line is a freight train containing numerous private owners wagons. No.4917 *Crosswood Hall* provides the haulage up the gradient. *Rail Archive Stephenson*

Left, above: **Snow Hill, 1950s**. A trio of up trains are depicted at the station, commencing with named express 'The Inter-City' headed by No.5032 *Usk Castle* in commendably clean condition. This train worked down from Paddington in the morning, taking 2 hours ten minutes to Birmingham, stopping only at High Wycombe. It went forward to Wolverhampton. The afternoon up train seen here took 5 minutes longer from Birmingham to London, but had two stops, Leamington Spa and High Wycombe. The LMR line between London Euston, Birmingham New Street and Wolverhampton High Level had a counterpart called 'The Midlander', which travelled up in the morning and down in the evening. *R S Carpenter collection*

Left: Collett 2-8-0 No.3849 has steam to spare as it goes along the platform line with a class H freight on 9 April 1958. The gradient into the station is noticeable.
B W L Brooksbank, Initial Photographics;

Left, below: Another clean engine, No.6014 *King Henry VII*, hauls an express from Wolverhampton into Snow Hill. With a 'King' on the front it is no doubt bound for London via High Wycombe. Some nice pointwork is visible in this shot. Like No.5032, No.6014 is a Wolverhampton Stafford Road based engine. *Author's collection*

Right, above: On the Northwood Street turntable in 1955 is No.4905 *Barton Hall*. While originally trains were stabled and made-up here, as early as 1900 this practice had to be moved to Bordesley, so congested was this site. Engines arriving from Tyseley ready for an up train would need turning in order to proceed. The sidings nearby were specially equipped for recharging gas wagons. The rebuilding of the GWR station in the city resulted in the resiting of the turntable from the west across the running lines to the east in New Yard in-between Water and Henrietta Streets.

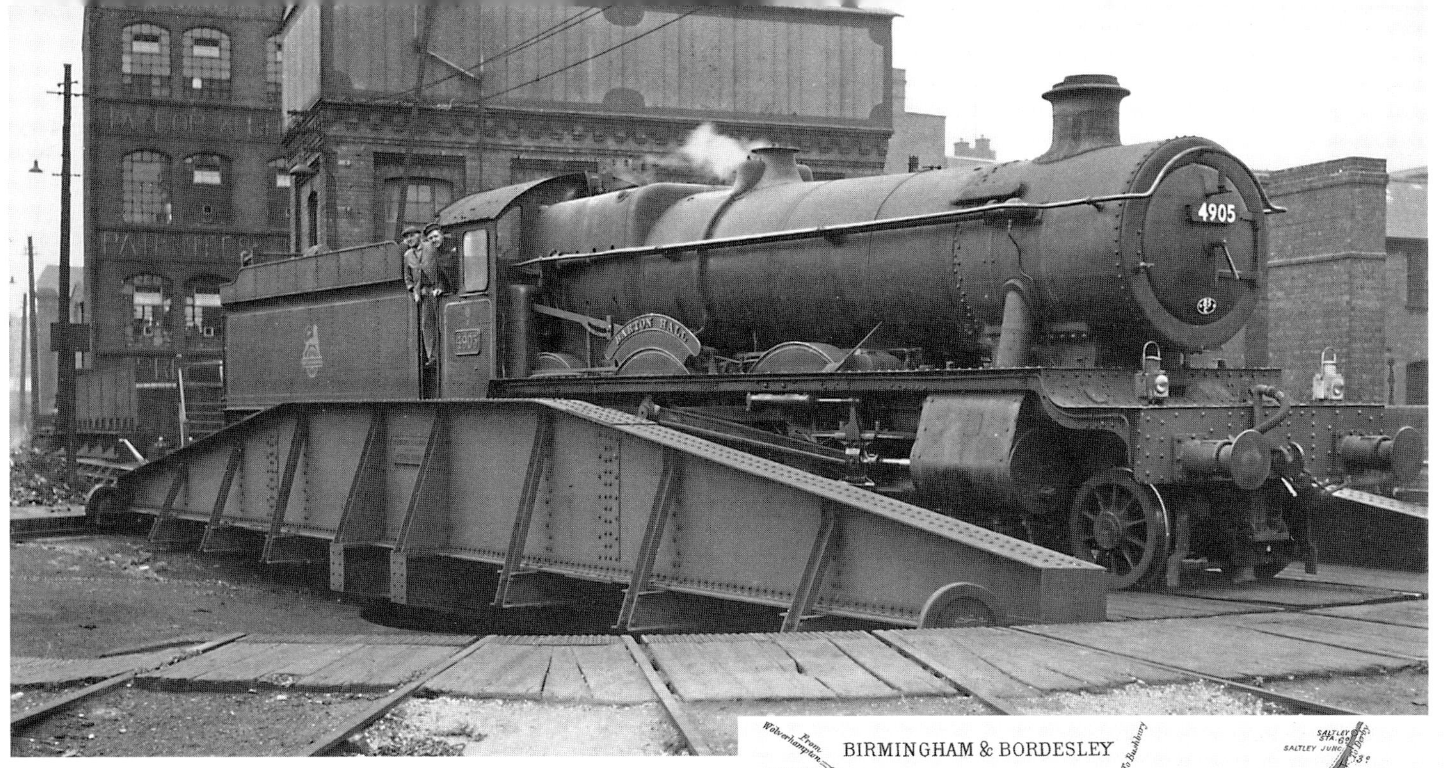

Right: **RCH diagram of Birmingham & Bordesley, 1914**.

Below: **Birmingham North Signal Box, 1915**. This box, perched some twenty feet above the lines was the product of the enlargement of the station and opened on 31 October 1909. From their commanding view the signalmen operated the 224 levers which were smaller than conventional ones as the points and signals were electrically operated. The track diagram of the box's area of responsibility is seen above. Communication with other boxes, both up and down, and instruments showing occupancy of the lines is provided by the apparatus on the shelf.

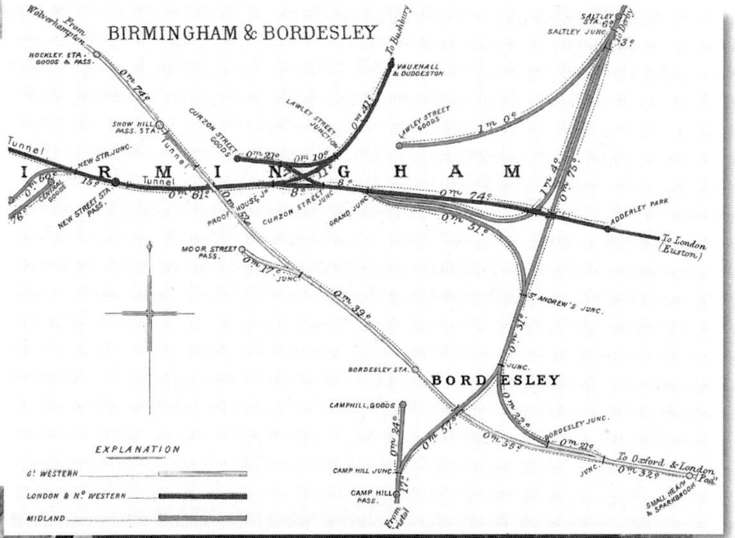

OXFORD-BIRMINGHAM GWR WORKING TIMETABLE JUNE 1862

Broad and Narrow Gauge - down trains - weekdays. Narrow gauge trains in bold

TRAIN	FROM	TO	OXFORD Arr	Dep	BIRMINGHAM Arr	Dep
Exp Goods	**10.45 pm London**	**Manchester**	**1.50 am**	**2.5 am**	**5.10 am**	**5.15 am**
Exp Goods	11.15 pm London	Wolverhampton	2.20 am	2.30 am	5.35 am	5.40 am
Goods	2.30 am Didcot	Wolverhampton	3.0 am	3.20 am	6.55 am	7.0 am
Coal empties	5.30 am Didcot	Wolverhampton	6.0 am	6.20 am	10.15 am	10.20 am
Goods	**5.20 am Basingstoke**	**Wolverhampton**	**7.15 am**	**7.40 am**	**11.48 am**	**11.50 am**
Passenger	6.0 am London	Wolverhampton	8.20 am	8.25 am	10.40 am	10.50 am
Goods	7.0 am Didcot	Wolverhampton	8.25 am	8.40 am	2.45 pm	2.46 pm
Passenger	7.30 am London	Wolverhampton	11.0 am	11.25 am	2.10 pm	2.20 pm
Passenger	**9.35 am London**	**Wolverhampton**	**11.10 am**	**11.15 am**	**12.55 pm**	**1.0 pm**
Coal	**10.50 am Reading**	**Wolverhampton**	**12.0 pm**	**12.15 pm**	**3.58 pm**	**4.0 pm**
Passenger	12 noon London	Wolverhampton	1.35 pm	1.38 pm	3.20 pm	3.30 pm
Passenger	2.0 pm London	Wolverhampton	4.0 pm	4.5 pm	6.35 pm	6.40 pm
Passenger	**3.40 pm London**	**Wolverhampton**	**5.17 pm**	**5.20 pm**	**7.5 pm**	**7.10 pm**
Passenger	4.50 pm London	Birmingham	6.35 pm	6.40 pm	9.50 pm	
Passenger	6.30 pm London	Wolverhampton	7.48 pm	7.50 pm	9.20 pm	9.30 pm

Notes: The 3.20 am departure starts from Oxford on Mondays.
The 7.15 am arrival will not run on Mondays unless required.
Goods from Oxford old station to Oxford at 8.35 am.
Some local Birmingham area workings not shown.

BIRMINGHAM-OXFORD GWR WORKING TIMETABLE JUNE 1862

Broad and Narrow Gauge - down trains - weekdays. Narrow gauge trains in bold

TRAIN	FROM	TO	BIRMINGHAM Arr	Dep	OXFORD Arr	Dep
Goods	8.50 pm Wolverhampton	Didcot	11.59 pm	12.0 am	3.15 am	3.30 am
Exp Goods	11.15 pm Wolverhampton	London		1.5 am	3.45 am	3.55 am
Goods	**Manchester**	**London**		**1.35 am**	**4.15 am**	**4.35 am**
Coal	**2.45 am Wolverhampton**	**Reading**		**4.30 am**	**7.40 am**	**7.50 am**
Passenger	6.20am Birmingham	London		6.20am	8.45am	9.30am
Passenger	7.0 am Wolverhampton	London	7.28 am	7.30 am	9.0 am	9.2 am
Goods	**5.20 am Wolverhampton**	**Basingstoke**		**8.5 am**	**12.25 pm**	**1.0 pm**
Passenger	9.10 am Wolverhampton	London	9.45 am	9.50 am	11.55 am	12 noon
Goods	8.25 am Wolverhampton	London	11.5 am	11.10 am	5.30 pm	6.0 pm
Passenger	11.29 am Wolverhampton	London	12.0 pm	12.10 pm	1.50 pm	1.55 pm
Passenger	**11.55 am Wolverhampton**	**London**	**12.45 pm**	**12.55 pm**	**3.45 pm**	**3.55 pm**
Passenger	**2.25pmWolverhampton**	**London**	**2.55pm**	**3.0pm**	**4.45pm**	**4.48pm**
Passenger	5.39 pm Wolverhampton	Didcot	6.25 pm	6.30 pm	8.50 pm	9.13 pm
Passenger	7.3 pm Wolverhampton	London	7.30 pm	7.35 pm	9.5 pm	9.8 pm
Coal	7.10 pm Wolverhampton	Didcot	8.19 pm	8.20 pm	11.45 pm	11.55 pm

Notes: The 3.15 am; 3.45 am; 4.15 am arrivals at Oxford do not run on Mondays.
The 12.25 pm arrival at Oxford will not run on Mondays unless required.
The 6.0 pm Oxford departure is from Oxford old station.
Goods from Oxford to Oxford old station at 8.15 pm.
Some local Birmingham area workings not shown.

BORDESLEY JUNCTION

UP Yards, total capacity of 1291 wagons

Baltic Yard
7 sidings, traffic for Gloucester, Cheltenham, Swindon Stores, Bristol and West, Swindon Transfer, Banbury Hump

Sorting Sidings
7 sidings for up and down traffic shunted off LMR

Reception roads connecting with LMR branch
3 reception lines and running round line for LMR engines

Baulks Yard
7 sidings, traffic for Leamington, North Warwickshire, Honeybourne, Tyseley, also Cripples

Pilot Line Sidings
3 sidings, traffic for Washwood Heath North, Small Heath and down side, Lawley Street

Old Yard
5 sidings, for down traffic

DOWN Yards, total capacity of 1366 wagons

Caledonia Yard
6 sidings, traffic for LMR, Oxley, Wednesbury, Bilston, Hockley, Scrap Dock

Small Heath Goods Yard
8 sidings for timber, heavy consignments, transhipments, Shed, scrap, inwards and outwards rough traffic

Field Traffic Sidings
4 sidings for LMR

Empty Shed
2 Side of Shed and Shed Road
2 Garden Roads

Traffic Sidings – North End
4 sidings for marshalling rough traffic off No. 6 Caledonia Sidings

Goods Mileage Yard – North End
2 sidings, Metal Shed and Bordesley traffic

Metal Shed Roads
3 sidings, inwards traffic

In 1955/56 five shunting engines worked seven days a week – one at Baltic Yard, up side; one at Baulks Yard, up side; one at Small Heath Yard and Down Side Bottom Yard; one at Old Yard, up side; one at Caledonia Sidings.

Gradient profiles

Special instructions in respect of gradients were issued for freight trains running between Leamington Spa, Warwick and Hatton, with assisting engines available as required. In some circumstances, the helper was attached in front of the train engine, rather than at the rear of the train. In respect of passenger trains requiring help on this section, the 'pilot' loco was usually coupled behind the train engine. For freights between Birmingham Moor Street and Snow Hill, any assisting engine was always at the front.

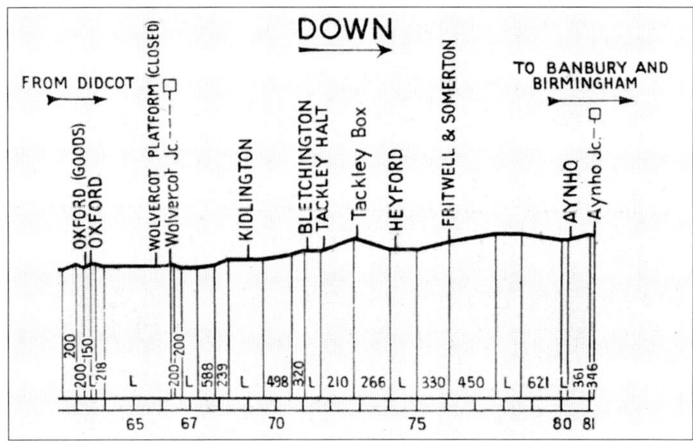

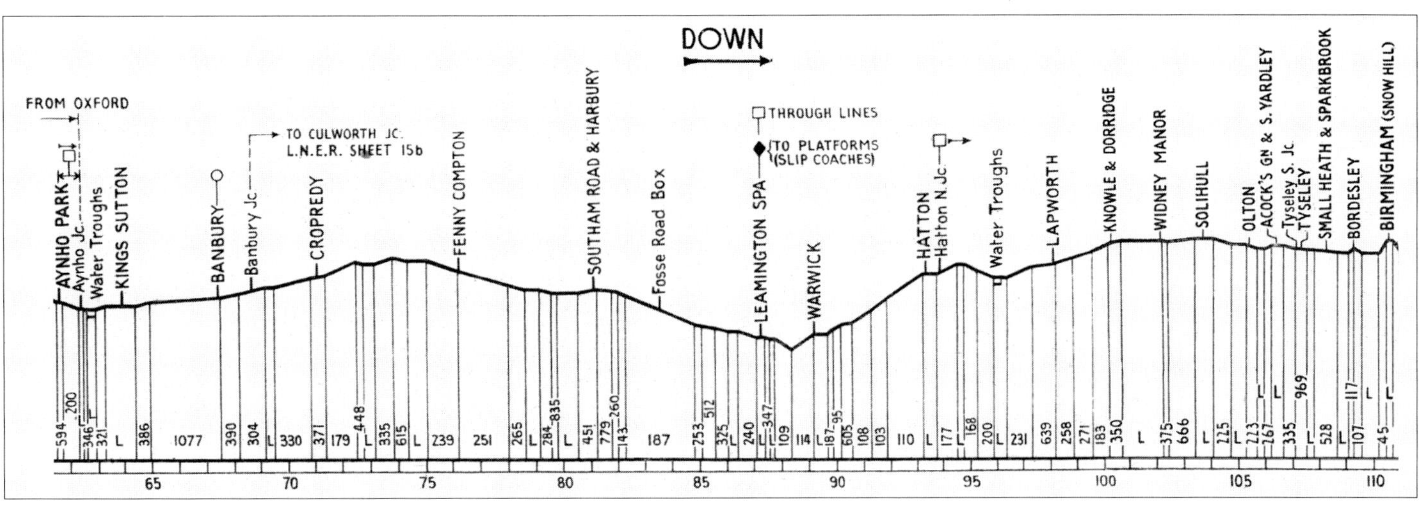

A blurry picture included due to its rarity value as it depicts the overall roof at Oxford GWR station, which was removed in 1890. Some ancient looking carriages lurk in the station. The pool of water in the foreground suggests that the rather splendidly attired gents are in danger of getting splashed!

Great Western Trust, courtesy Laurence Waters

Acknowledgements
With much of the railway infrastructure of the original route still in place one would have thought that evidence to illustrate the history of the line would be straightforward. Whilst in many instances this has been true, as always there are several, usually industrial, undertakings that may as well have never existed with little or no photographic proof available. In spite of generous help from the staff and extensive use of public and private libraries in Oxford, Banbury, Leamington and Birmingham I was unable to discover illustrations of some features. The most grievous of these concern the train shed at Leamington and the exciting practice of slipping coaches along the line. I am very grateful to Audie Baker at Kidderminster Railway Museum for his time, support and suggestions as well as the continuous help and friendship from Stephen Mourton at Runpast Publishing. While every effort has been made to obtain permission from owners of copyright materials contained herein, I would like to apologise for any omissions and would be pleased to correct matters in any future editions.

Bibliography
There were several books that assisted me including Derek Harrison's titles on Snow Hill; Laurence Waters' on Oxford; Alan Bennett's *Great Western Lines & Landscapes*; J H Russell's *Banbury & Cheltenham Railway*; R A Cooke's *Track Layout Diagrams of the GWR and BR WR*. Many other books, magazines and articles too numerous to list were consulted as well as booklets from railway societies and their members.

Related titles from Runpast Publishing:

Oxford Worcester & Wolverhampton Portrait of a Famous Route – **Part One**: Oxford to Worcester

Oxford Worcester & Wolverhampton Portrait of a Famous Route – **Part Two**: Worcester to Wolverhampton

Birmingham-Bristol Portrait of a Famous Midland Route **Part One**: Birmingham to Cheltenham

Birmingham-Bristol Portrait of a Famous Midland Route **Part Two**: Cheltenham to Bristol and Bath

Birmingham-Derby Portrait of a Famous Route